When the Cold Wind Blows

BARB ADAMS & ALMA ALLEN OF BLACKBIRD DESIGNS

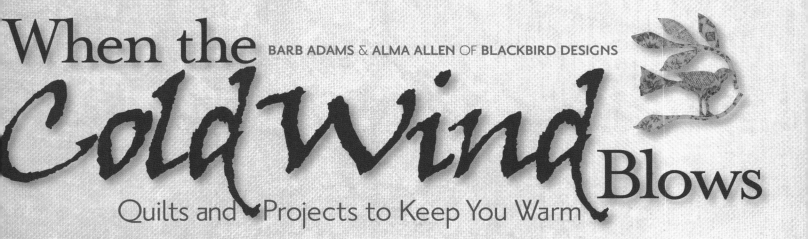

Quilts and Projects to Keep You Warm

When the Cold Wind Blows
Quilts and Projects to Keep You Warm

By Barb Adams & Alma Allen of Blackbird Designs
Editor: Kent Richards
Technical Editors: Kathe Dougherty and Jane Miller
Book Design: Amy Robertson
Photography: Aaron T. Leimkuehler
Illustration: Lon Eric Craven and Eric Sears
Production assistance: Jo Ann Groves

Published by:
Kansas City Star Books
1729 Grand Blvd.
Kansas City, Missouri, USA 64108
All rights reserved
Copyright©2008 The Kansas City Star Co. and Blackbird Designs

First edition, first printing
978-1-933466-78-1
Printed in the United States of America
by Walsworth Publishing Co., Marceline, MO

Library of Congress Control Number: 2008938325

To order copies, call StarInfo at
(816) 234-4636 and say "Books."
www.pickledish.com

Table of *Contents*

Introduction 4
Acknowledgements 5
Hand Appliqué Instructions 6

Winter Garden & Love Letters

Before You Begin 7
Winter Garden Supply List 9
Love Letters Supply List 11
Winter Garden Picture 12
Love Letters Picture 13

The 9 Blocks

The Hedge Apple 14
The Bur Oak Leaf 16
The Winter Rose 18
The Coxcomb 20
The Rose Hip 22
The Holly Leaf 24
The Ornamental Kale 26
The Winter Wreath 28
The Pomegranate 30

Templates and Diagrams

Urn 33
The Hedge Apple 34
The Bur Oak Leaf 36
The Winter Rose 39
The Coxcomb 42
The Rose Hip 45
The Holly Leaf 48
The Ornamental Kale 50
The Winter Wreath 53
The Pomegranate 56

Christmas at Kindred Spirit Place

Ginger and Ron Schrader's Home 59

Other Quilts and Projects

Autumn Thistle 66
Trick or Treat 72
Garden Song 76
Harvest Basket 78
Goldenrod in Bloom 84
Birds and Old Buttons Pillow 92
Holly and Mistletoe 96
Frost on the Ferns 106
'Back to School' Pillow Sham 112
Rose Hip Hooked Rug 116

Introduction

In the nation's heartland autumn's arrival brings a breath of fresh crisp air. The oppressive heat of summer begins to abate and work in the garden begins to slow. The brilliant colors of the leaves herald the change of seasons. We begin to work more inside our homes. The world becomes quieter, nights become longer and winter approaches. Stars in the clear night sky sparkle. As frost and snow begin to cover our world, it's time to bring out the blankets and quilts as we snuggle up to keep warm. Now we have the time to dream of new quilts and projects to keep us busy during the long winter evenings. This time of the year, when the cold wind blows, is one of our favorites.

Our featured quilts, "Winter Garden" and "Love Letters" have nine large blocks using some of our favorite plants and flowers that remind us of autumn and winter seasons. The large shapes in each 28" block are easy to appliqué. Both quilts show different color and placement options. Barb's "Winter Garden" quilt has soft colors. Her blocks are arranged in a vintage way. You see an upright block no matter where you stand in your bedroom. Mine, "Love Letters," was arranged with all the urns upright. My colors are stronger and the contrast is more pronounced against the background fabric.

If arranged as Barb's were, the pattern began to move visually as your eyes try to find a place to rest. It was too busy. To calm things down a bit, I arranged the urns all upright lending a more formal structure. However you decide to do this quilt, I know you will enjoy it as much as I did. I called Barb and told her after I completed each block, "I can't believe how fun these are to do!"

As you glance through the book, take a look at the bindings on these quilts. You will notice we are in our "rick rack" phase of life. Not a bad place to be either. The rick rack gives a scalloped edge to the quilts without having to add borders.

We include a visit to Ginger and Ron Schrader's home as they decorate for Christmas. Ginger loves the look of primitives and antiques blended together. Her simple way of celebrating with treasured collections and fresh greenery will inspire you this holiday season. Her love of nature is shown throughout her home.

Barb's "Trick or Treat" quilt is perfect for the autumn months and her "Holly and Mistletoe" is the one you will want your guests to sleep under during the Christmas season. We hope at least one of these projects or quilts will be the one you will want to complete as the cold wind begins to blow. —Alma Allen

Acknowledgements

This book would not have been possible without the contributions of many.

Barb and I love to showcase our friends' homes to you in these publications. We owe much to Ginger and Ron Schrader of Kansas City, Missouri. They welcomed us into their home on a very snowy day and shared their holiday spirit. We hope you find inspiration in their home and their natural style of decorating.

We know you will love the soft, scrappy, color palette of the "Rose Hips" hooked rug done by Johnna Perdue. Her warm folk art style of hooking would be cherished in any home.

Kelli Trimble, of Moda Fabrics, sewed the quilt "Harvest Home" for us. The quilting was done by Maggi Honeyman. Their lovely work is a welcome addition to this book.

A friend makes the work go faster. Jean Stanclift stepped in and helped me appliqué four of my "Love Letter" blocks. I couldn't have made the deadline without her.

Quilts would never be the same without the added texture and design of the quilting stitch. Jeanne Zyck's quilting designs always reflect and enhance our patterns.

Many hours of time must be devoted to bring projects to completion. The sewing skills of Leona Adams are essential to this endeavor. After you see the "Trick or Treat" quilt she sewed, you will know she must really love her daughter Barb.

My friend Cherie Ralston came over for an afternoon of sewing. Her inspiration gave me the idea for the border design of my "Autumn Thistle" quilt. Where would we be without our friends?

Many thanks to my husband David Allen, who takes the time to read over the text and does my first edit. His technical writing skills are much better than mine and two heads are always better than one.

Our photographer, Aaron Leimkuehler, has captured the beauty of our friend's home and quilts through the eye of the camera. It's always a pleasure to work on a project with Aaron.

The talents of Eric Sears and L. Eric Craven are essential to this project. Their skills in illustrating the diagrams and patterns bring clarity to the instructions.

Alissa Christianson graphs our cross-stitch patterns. There is a real artistry in using the symbols to shade the design, making it easy to count and stitch.

The beautiful book design by Amy Robertson binds our efforts into a compelling format. Her vision of the book illuminates our theme.

Photographs must be color-corrected for printing and Jo Ann Groves works in a very small, dark office accomplishing this magic. Any loose threads or problems are digitally corrected by Jo Ann. A standing ovation to you Jo Ann for making the rick rack binding look great.

No one wants mistakes in their quilting books. Kathe Dougherty and Jane Miller reviewed every pattern to make sure there is enough fabric, the correct number of pieces are cut and we are consistent and accurate with our instructions. The knowledge of these women is essential to this project.

Many thanks go to our editor, Kent Richards. Kent brings clear, concise instructions through his editing skills. His coordination of the entire process makes everything easy. We couldn't do this without his help.

Finally, thanks belong to you for your continued support and kindness. We hope our friends' creative ideas, the pictures captured by Aaron Leimkuehler, quilt patterns and projects will bring you inspiration and hours of pleasure. —A.A.

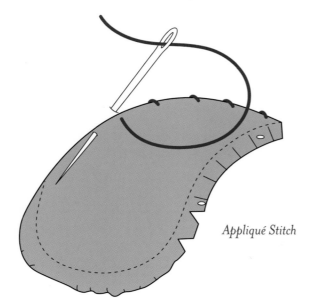

Appliqué Stitch

Hand Appliqué Instructions

❀ Make templates of the appliqué shapes using freezer paper or plastic template material. Do not add any seam allowance to these shapes.

❀ If using plastic, trace around the templates on the right side of your fabric. Use a marking pencil that will be easy to see on your fabric. This drawn line indicates your seam line. To cut reversed pieces, flip the plastic template over and trace the reversed shape to the right side of the fabric. If using freezer paper, first trace the shapes onto the dull side of the paper. Iron the paper templates, shiny side down, onto the right side of the fabric. Trace around the template. Peel the paper template away carefully, as it can be reused. For a reversed piece, trace on the shiny side of the paper.

❀ After the seam line has been drawn on the right side of the fabric, cut out the shapes, adding a 1/8" - 1/4" seam allowance.

❀ Fold the background fabric in half vertically and horizontally. Finger-press the folds. Open the fabric.

❀ To help achieve placement of the design, refer to the block diagram located with the templates. A one-inch grid was added to each diagram to indicate position for the pieces. If you look closely at each quilt block, you will notice each is unique. The pieces were placed on the block in a whimsical fashion.

❀ Center the design on the background block using the fold lines and placement diagram as a guide.

❀ Baste the shapes into place on the background block with glue stick or appliqué pins. Larger shapes require basting stitches to hold the shapes in place securely.

❀ Use thread that matches your appliqué piece, not the background. Use a two-ply, cotton thread that is 50-60 weight.

❀ Cut the thread length about 12" -15". Longer lengths of thread may become worn and break as you stitch.

❀ For concave curves (curves that go in) clip to the seam line, then turn under the seam allowance. This will allow the fabric to lie flat. Convex curves (or curves that go out) do not require clipping.

❀ Sew the pieces that will be covered by another piece first. For example, sew the stems first. Next, sew the flower or leaf that covers the end of the stem.

❀ Using the point and edge of your needle, turn under the fabric on the drawn seam line and appliqué the shape to the background fabric. Try to achieve about 7-9 stitches per inch.

Winter Garden & Love Letters

Before You Begin

As the weather begins to cool, our thoughts turn to quilting. These nine large appliqué blocks each highlight autumn and winter motifs that we love.

Barb and I have each completed the same blocks, but with different color schemes. The blocks have been stitched together two different ways as well. Barb's has been sewn together in an old fashioned way. The soft colors of her quilt need the visual interest of her setting design. The eye lingers longer to find the pattern. The bolder contrast of my colors need to be calmed down a bit. Setting each urn upright gave mine a more formal and "less busy" look and gives the eye a place to rest. To decide which version you would like to make refer to pages 12 and 13.

When we begin a project, we know we don't have the time to do it by hand. We use an Invisible Machine Appliqué method. Unlike hand appliqué, each template is drawn on the slick side of the freezer paper. For the reverse template, each template is drawn on the dull side of the paper. If we need multiples of one template, we cut up to six at a time by drawing one piece and layering it with six sheets of freezer paper. Stapling them together prevents the papers from slipping as you cut out the templates. Each piece in the quilt block will need a template, except for the bias tape. After all the pieces are cut out, we iron the slick side of the paper to the reverse side of the fabric. We then cut out each piece, adding our seam allowance as we cut. We use glue stick to glue the seam allowance to the paper template. When complete, each piece "looks" finished. We use Roxanne's Glue-Baste-It to dot the seam allowance and then position each piece on the background block.

We use a cotton thread for the appliqué. The most important step is to match your sewing thread to the appliqué piece. A well-matched thread hides the stitches. Use the blind hemstitch on your sewing machine. The stitch pattern you want is one that has several straight stitches and then a zigzag stitch. The stitch width should be just wide enough to catch a couple of threads of the appliqué piece. The zigzag stitches need to be 1/16" - 1/8" apart. Practice on a scrap piece of fabric until you are comfortable with the stitch length and width.

After the pieces are stitched in place on the background block, turn the block over to the reverse side. Cut away the fabric from under each appliquéd piece leaving a 1/4" seam allowance. Dampen the block with cool water and wait about 5 minutes for the glue to release. Pull the fabric on the diagonal both ways and the freezer paper will pop loose. Remove all the paper from each block.

This method is not relaxing like hand stitching, but it does reduce the time needed to complete each block. Barb and I were able to complete our quilts "Winter Garden" and "Love Letters" in about a week's time. (Of course, that means you're working on the blocks about 10 hours a day.) This method gives you more time to sleep under the quilt and dream of your next project.

After You Finish

Refer to the pictures on pages 12 and 13 to help with placement and sew your blocks together.

The rick rack is dyed with liquid Rit tan dye. Combine 8 cups of warm water with 1/4 cup of liquid Rit tan dye. Add 4 tablespoons of salt. Add the rick rack to the dye bath and mix well to dye the rick rack evenly. Leave the rick rack in the dye bath for about 15 minutes. Check the rick rack after this time. The rick rack will look a shade lighter when it is dry. When you are pleased with the results, remove the rick rack from the dye bath and rinse it until the water runs clear. Air dry the rick rack.

The quilt must be quilted before the rick rack can be sewn in place. Baste the rick rack along the right side of the quilt top, continuing around each edge. Add a bit of extra rick rack as you baste around each corner. Clip if needed. When you come back to the place you began, fold the raw rick rack edges over into the seam allowance and overlap the rick rack a bit.

Cut bias strips 1 1/2" wide. Sew them together until you have 9 1/2 yds. Use this strip for your binding. Sew the binding in place, right side of the strip facing the right side of the quilt top. The rick rack will be sandwiched between the quilt top and the binding. Fold the binding over to the back of the quilt, turn under a seam allowance and whip stitch in place.

Winter Garden

Project Size 84" x 84" • Block Size 28" finished

Supply List

For Barb's Quilt "Winter Garden"

For backgrounds

- 2 1/2 yds. large tan pillar print
- 1 2/3 yds. each of two different tan tone-on-tone prints
- 1 yd. each of two different tan tone-on-tone prints

For appliqué pieces

The fabric numbers refer to "Harvest Home" line of fabric by Blackbird Designs for Moda Fabrics.
- 1/2 yd. each of 4 different purple-kale prints
  (2621-17, 2626-17, 2624-17 & 2625-17)
- 1/4 yd., each of 5 different hedge-apple green prints
  (2620-15, 2626-15, 2625-15, 2621-15 & 2624-15)
- 1/4 yd. each of 4 different rosehip-red prints
  (2621-16, 2620-16, 2626-16 & 2627-16)
- 1/4 yd. each of 6 different bark-brown prints
  (2626-12, 2621-12, 2623-12, 2627-12, 2625-12 & 2629-12)
- 3/4 yd. for binding
- 9 1/2 yds. jumbo rick rack 1" white
  (United Notions 454 M & J Trimming)
- 1 bottle Rit dye #16 tan
- 3/8" Clover bias tape maker
- 1/2" Clover bias tape maker
- Freezer paper for templates

Opposite page:

Winter Garden

Barb's Quilt

Design by Barb Adams

Appliqué by Leona Adams

Quilting design by Jeanne Zyck

Love Letters

Project Size 84" x 84" ◆ Block Size 28" finished

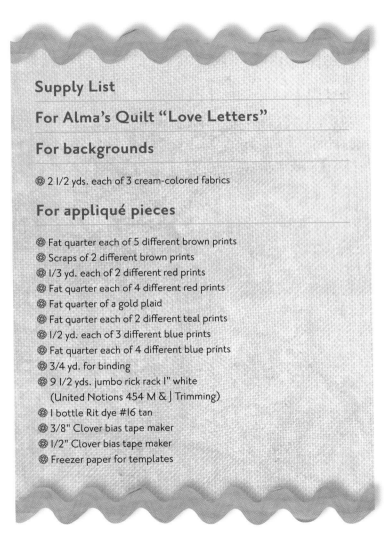

Supply List

For Alma's Quilt "Love Letters"

For backgrounds

- 2 1/2 yds. each of 3 cream-colored fabrics

For appliqué pieces

- Fat quarter each of 5 different brown prints
- Scraps of 2 different brown prints
- 1/3 yd. each of 2 different red prints
- Fat quarter each of 4 different red prints
- Fat quarter of a gold plaid
- Fat quarter each of 2 different teal prints
- 1/2 yd. each of 3 different blue prints
- Fat quarter each of 4 different blue prints
- 3/4 yd. for binding
- 9 1/2 yds. jumbo rick rack 1" white
  (United Notions 454 M & J Trimming)
- 1 bottle Rit dye #16 tan
- 3/8" Clover bias tape maker
- 1/2" Clover bias tape maker
- Freezer paper for templates

Opposite page:

Love Letters

Alma's Quilt

Design by Barb Adams

Appliqué by Jean Stanclift and Alma Allen

Quilting design by Jeanne Zyck

Winter Garden

Barb Adams

Love Letters

Alma Allen

The Hedge Apple

The Osage Orange or Hedge Apple is covered with long thorns, so care must be taken when picking the fruit of this tree. The hedge apples are large green wrinkled balls and are produced only on the female tree. Hedge apples can be up to 6" in diameter. Gather them in a basket or urn, add autumn leaves and display them on your porch to celebrate the season.

Osage Orange trees were planted in rows, pruned to encourage thick growth and used for fencing before the invention of barbed wire. The thorns and thick growth were enough to contain farm animals. These fence lines can still be found along old country roads.

Instructions

Cutting measurements include a 1/4" seam allowance.

❀ Cut 9 - 28 1/2" squares from the background prints. This will be enough for all of the blocks.

❀ Make 6 1/2 yds. of the 3/8" bias tape and 11 yds of the 1/2" bias tape for the flower stems. This will be enough for all 9 blocks. The wreath block uses 5/8 yd. of 1/2" bias tape. The remaining flower blocks each use about 3/4 yd. of 3/8" bias tape and 1 1/4 yds. of 1/2" bias tape.

The Hedge Apple

❀ Locate the placement diagram on page 34. Note the templates needed for this block. The templates are located on pages 33 and 35. Refer to the photo for color placement.

❀ Cut the 3/8" and 1/2" bias tape needed for the hedge apple stems.

❀ Cut out the shapes, adding a 1/8" - 1/4" seam allowance. Refer to the diagram and baste the pieces in place on the background fabric.

❀ Appliqué the pieces to the background.

The Bur Oak Leaf

The bark of the Bur Oak is rough with deep ridges and gives it a shaggy appearance. The Bur Oak lives for 200 to 400 years and grows 50 to 80 feet tall. The leaves of a Bur Oak are large with rounded lobes. The large, heavily fringed caps of the acorn are distinctive and perfect to collect for an autumn display.

Instructions

The Bur Oak Leaf

❀ Locate the placement diagram on page 36. Note the templates needed for this block. The templates are located on pages 33, 37 and 38. Refer to the photo for color placement.

❀ Cut the 3/8" and 1/2" bias tape needed for the leaf stems.

❀ Cut out the shapes, adding a 1/8" - 1/4" seam allowance. Refer to the diagram and baste the pieces in place on the background fabric.

❀ Appliqué the pieces to the background.

The Winter Rose

Widely grown for their beauty and fragrance, the rose is symbolic of love. Although the perennial shrub is armed with thorns, the flowers with their heady fragrance and lovely bloom make it all worthwhile.

Instructions

The Winter Rose

- Locate the placement diagram on page 39. Note the templates needed for this block. The templates are located on pages 33, 40 and 41. Refer to the photo for color placement.

- Cut the 3/8" and 1/2" bias tape needed for the flower stems.

- Cut out the shapes, adding a 1/8" - 1/4" seam allowance. Refer to the diagram and baste the pieces in place on the background fabric.

- Appliqué the pieces to the background.

The Coxcomb

The Coxcomb is a tender annual species whose unusual flower head is enlarged and flattened like a fan or cockscomb. These flowers look and feel like velvet. They are available in deep, rich colors.

Instructions

The Coxcomb

🌸 Locate the placement diagram on page 42. Note the templates needed for this block. The templates are located on pages 33, 43 and 44. Refer to the photo for color placement.

🌸 Cut the 3/8" and 1/2" bias tape needed for the flower stems.

🌸 Cut out the shapes, adding a 1/8" - 1/4" seam allowance. Refer to the diagram and baste the pieces in place on the background fabric.

🌸 Appliqué the pieces to the background.

The Rose Hip

After the bloom has faded away, the rose is not finished with its display. Early in the fall the rose hips are formed after the bloom is spent. If you prune away the faded bloom you will miss seeing the fruit.

Rose hips are high in vitamin C and are edible. Harvest your rose hips after the first frost. Frost helps sweeten the flavor. Pick rose hips that are firm and have good color. Leave the shriveled or dried hips for the birds.

Instructions

The Rose Hip

- Locate the placement diagram on page 45. Note the templates needed for this block. The templates are located on pages 33, 46 and 47. Refer to the photo for color placement.

- Cut the 3/8" and 1/2" bias tape needed for the flower stems.

- Cut out the shapes, adding a 1/8" - 1/4" seam allowance. Refer to the diagram and baste the pieces in place on the background fabric.

- Appliqué the pieces to the background.

The Holly Leaf

The Holly tree can grow to 50 feet. Its white, star–shaped flowers bloom in the spring. In the fall the female plant bears red berries, which will last throughout the winter season. The plant is an evergreen, as the holly leaves remain on the plant throughout the winter. For this reason the plant represents immortality.

Bring cuttings inside during the winter months. The rich green leaves accented with red berries add color and warmth to the holidays.

Instructions

The Holly Leaf

- Locate the placement diagram on page 48. Note the templates needed for this block. The templates are located on pages 33 and 49. Refer to the photo for color placement.

- Cut the 3/8" and 1/2" bias tape needed for the leaf stems.

- Cut out the shapes, adding a 1/8" - 1/4" seam allowance. Refer to the diagram and baste the pieces in place on the background fabric.

- Appliqué the pieces to the background.

The Ornamental Kale

Ornamental kale is a popular addition to the fall garden. Its beautiful leaves become more colorful after the first frost. As it grows, the leaves unfold and create a round leafy rosette shape. When planted as a border or used in a container garden, kale adds rugged beauty. As autumn's chill begins to discourage most plants' growth, kale begins to shine, adding beauty, color and pleasing shapes to the garden.

Instructions

The Ornamental Kale

❀ Locate the placement diagram on page 50. Note the templates needed for this block. The templates are located on pages 33, 51 and 52. Refer to the photo for color placement.

❀ Cut the 3/8" and 1/2" bias tape needed for the flower stems.

❀ Cut out the shapes, adding a 1/8" - 1/4" seam allowance. Refer to the diagram and baste the pieces in place on the background fabric.

❀ Appliqué the pieces to the background.

The Winter Wreath

Nothing is more welcoming than a wreath on the front door. Soft boughs of greenery break up the geometric lines of the door and offer a warm and comfortable look to your home. Wreaths are used to celebrate each season of the year. Evergreens are often used in winter wreaths. Their lush green foliage and fresh scent are a welcome relief to the cold and dark season. The green colors remind us that spring and warmer weather is not too far away. Wreaths also symbolize remembrance and the circle of life. For this reason they are often left at the gravesites of loved ones.

Instructions

The Winter Wreath Block

🏵 Locate the placement diagram on page 53. Note the templates needed for this block. The templates are located on pages 54 and 55. Refer to the photo for color placement.

🏵 Cut the 1/2" bias tape needed for the flower stems.

🏵 Cut the wreath template from freezer paper. Cut a 9" square from your wreath fabric. Fold it into fourths and position the ends of the freezer paper template on the folds. Iron the template in place. Cut out the wreath, adding a 1/8" - 1/4" seam allowance.

🏵 Cut out the shapes, adding a 1/8" - 1/4" seam allowance. Refer to the diagram and baste the pieces in place on the background fabric.

🏵 Appliqué the pieces to the background.

The Pomegranate

Pomegranates were introduced to America by the Spaniards. They are harvested from a small, deciduous tree growing about 25 feet in height. In the spring they have large, red-orange tinted flowers. The foliage is dark green. The profusion of lovely red seeds makes the pomegranate a symbol of fertility, birth, abundance and eternal life. Legend says that the pomegranate tree was the "tree of life" in the Garden of Eden.

Use the beautiful seeds as a garnish in a spinach salad this winter. These crunchy colorful seeds are bursting with flavor.

Instructions

The Pomegranate

⚜ Locate the placement diagram on page 56. Note the templates needed for this block. The templates are located on pages 33, 57 and 58. Refer to the photo for color placement.

⚜ Cut the 3/8" and 1/2" bias tape needed for the flower stems.

⚜ Cut out the shapes, adding a 1/8" - 1/4" seam allowance. Refer to the diagram and baste the pieces in place on the background fabric.

⚜ Appliqué the pieces to the background.

Templates and Diagrams
for Winter Garden and Love Letters

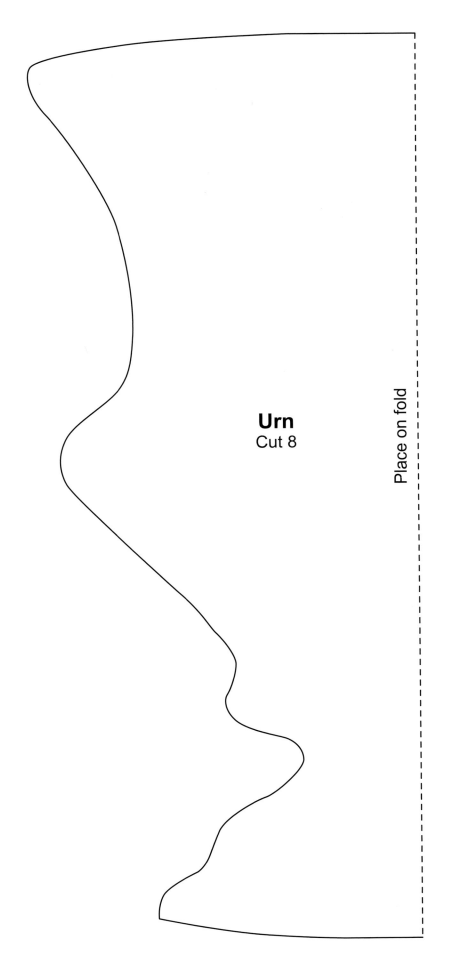

Urn
Cut 8

Place on fold

The Hedge Apple

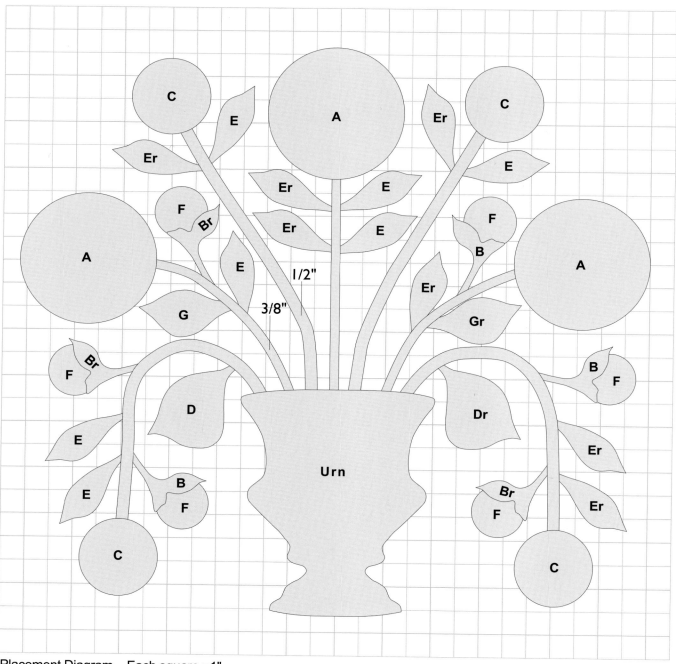

Placement Diagram – Each square =1"

The 3/8" and 1/2" stems are consistently placed throughout the 8 urn blocks.

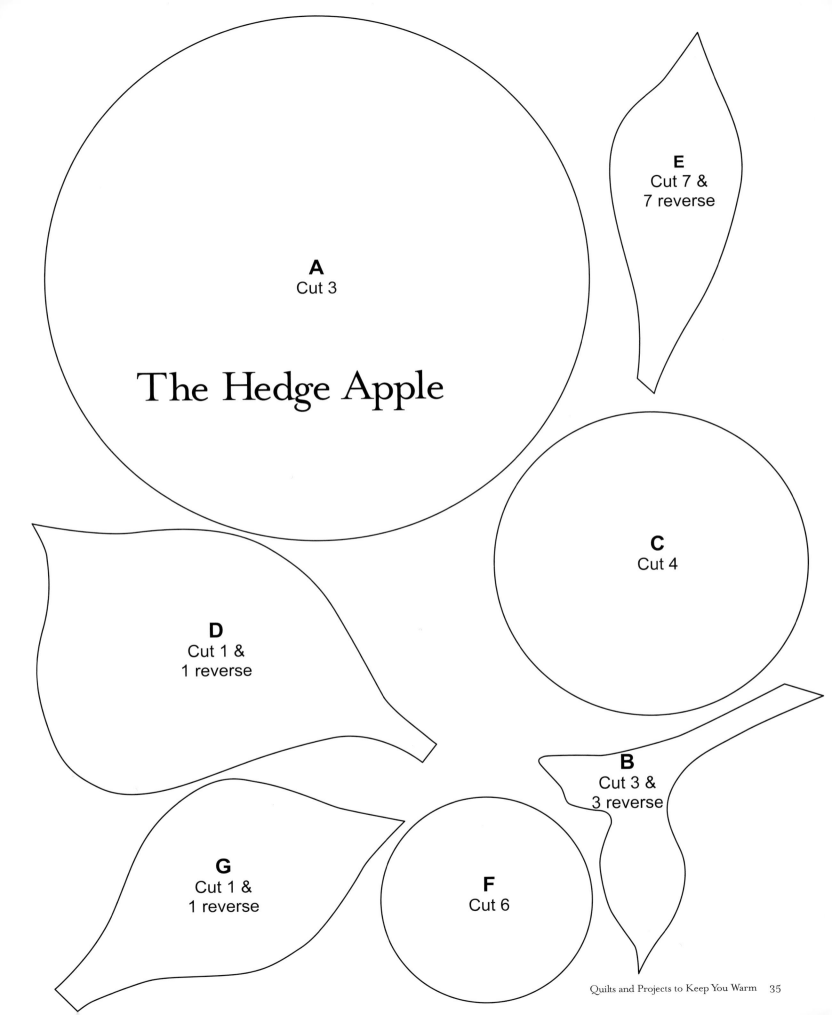

A
Cut 3

The Hedge Apple

E
Cut 7 &
7 reverse

C
Cut 4

D
Cut 1 &
1 reverse

B
Cut 3 &
3 reverse

G
Cut 1 &
1 reverse

F
Cut 6

The Bur Oak Leaf

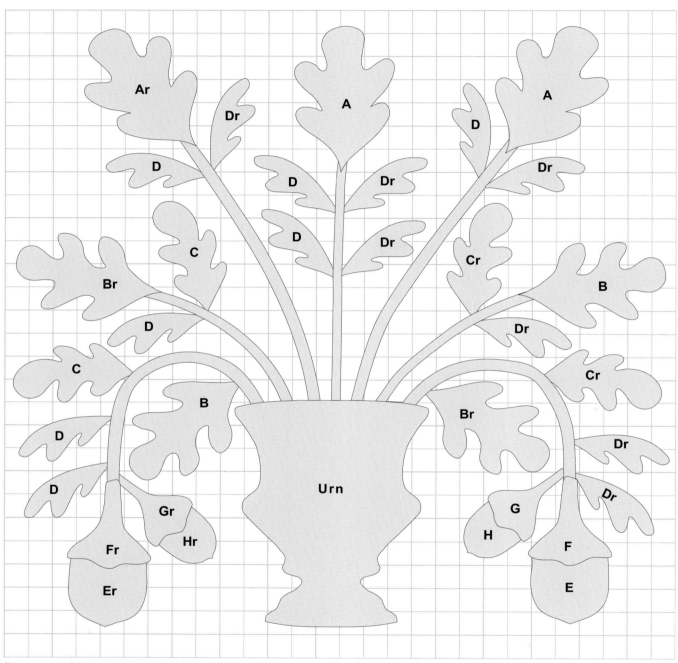

Placement Diagram – Each square =1"

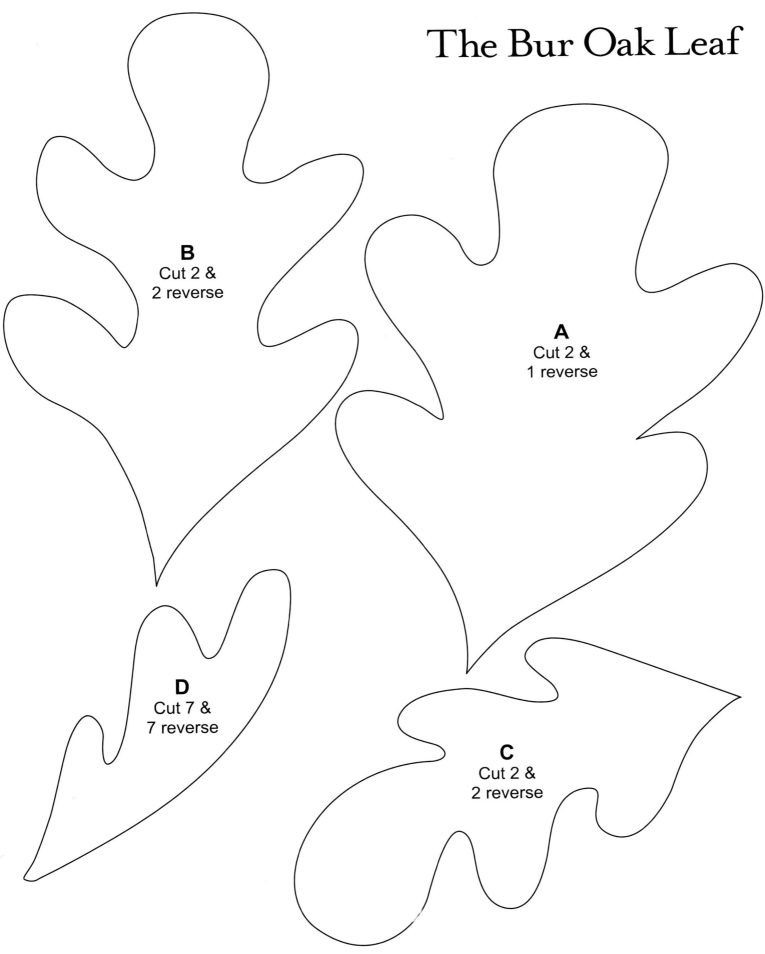

The Bur Oak Leaf

B
Cut 2 &
2 reverse

A
Cut 2 &
1 reverse

D
Cut 7 &
7 reverse

C
Cut 2 &
2 reverse

The Bur Oak Leaf

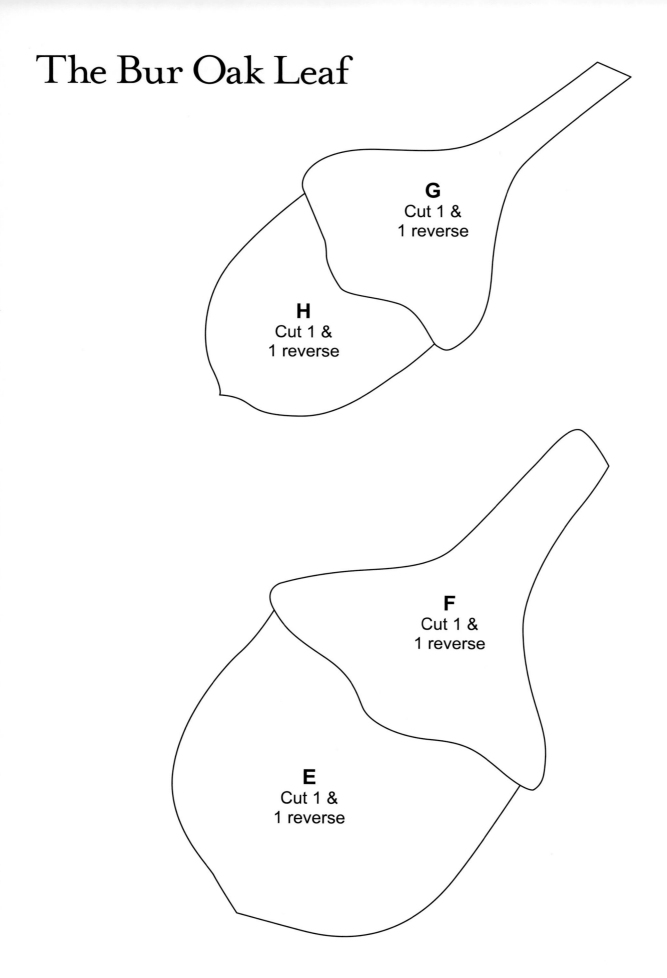

G
Cut 1 &
1 reverse

H
Cut 1 &
1 reverse

F
Cut 1 &
1 reverse

E
Cut 1 &
1 reverse

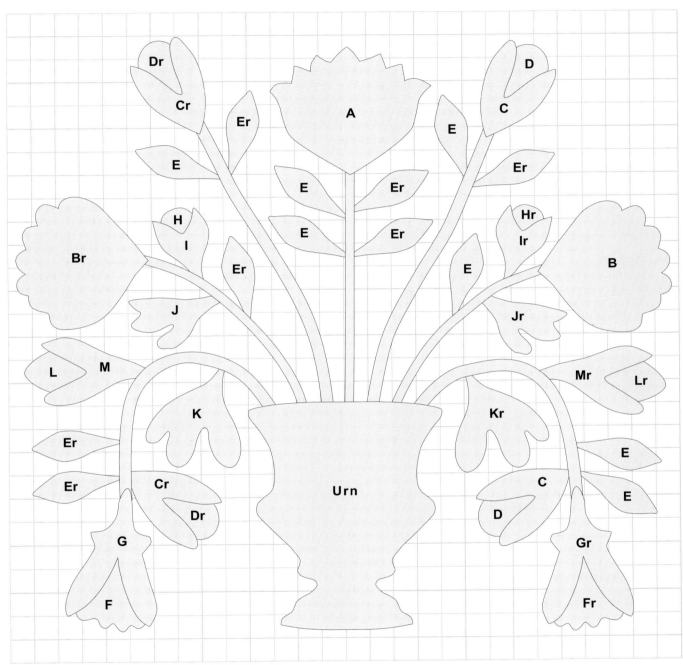

Placement Diagram — Each square =1"

The Winter Rose

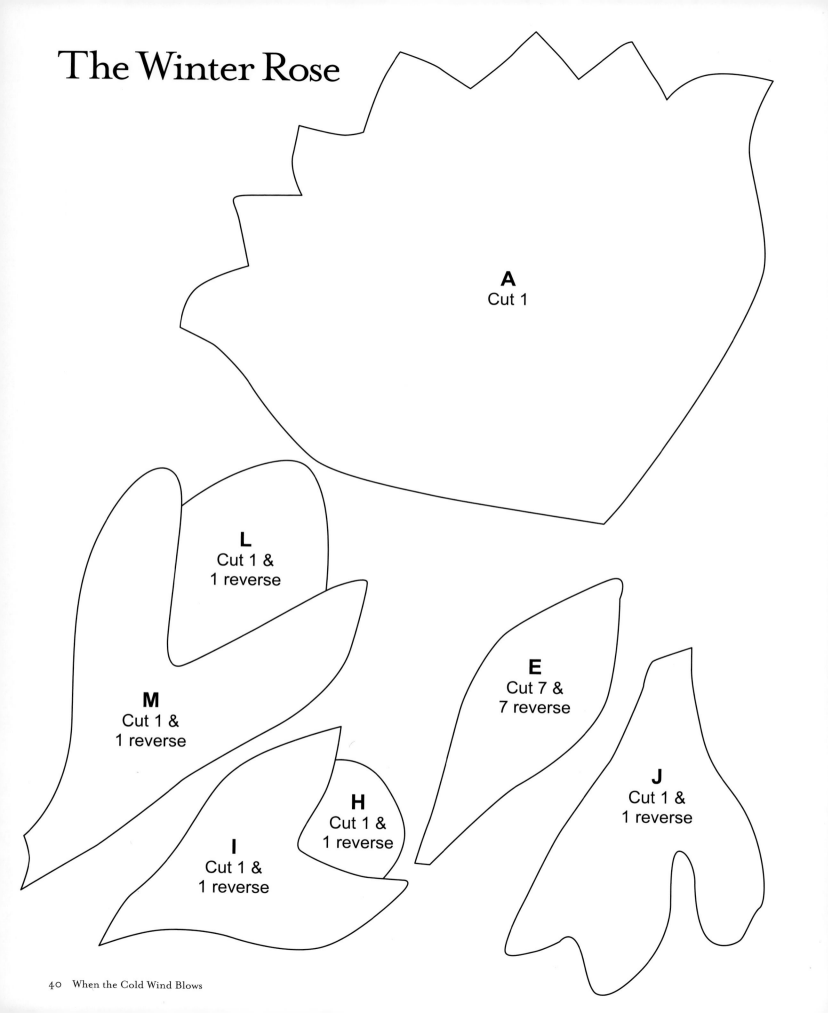

A
Cut 1

L
Cut 1 &
1 reverse

M
Cut 1 &
1 reverse

E
Cut 7 &
7 reverse

J
Cut 1 &
1 reverse

H
Cut 1 &
1 reverse

I
Cut 1 &
1 reverse

The Winter Rose

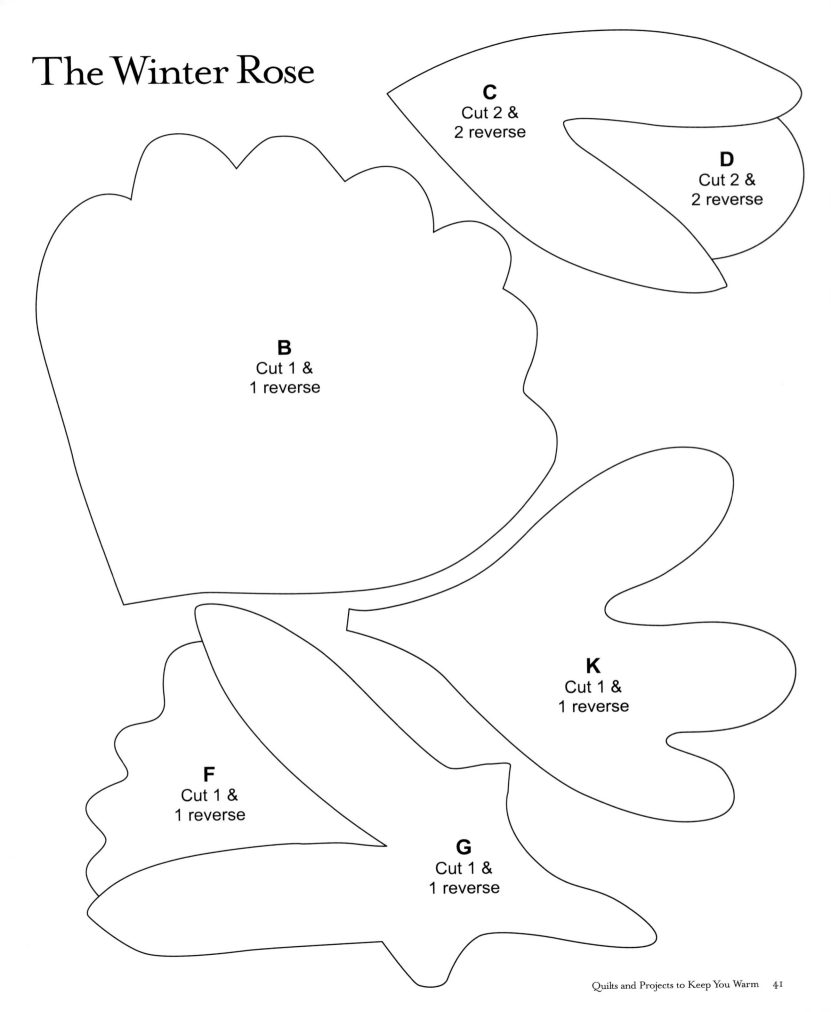

C
Cut 2 &
2 reverse

D
Cut 2 &
2 reverse

B
Cut 1 &
1 reverse

K
Cut 1 &
1 reverse

F
Cut 1 &
1 reverse

G
Cut 1 &
1 reverse

The Coxcomb

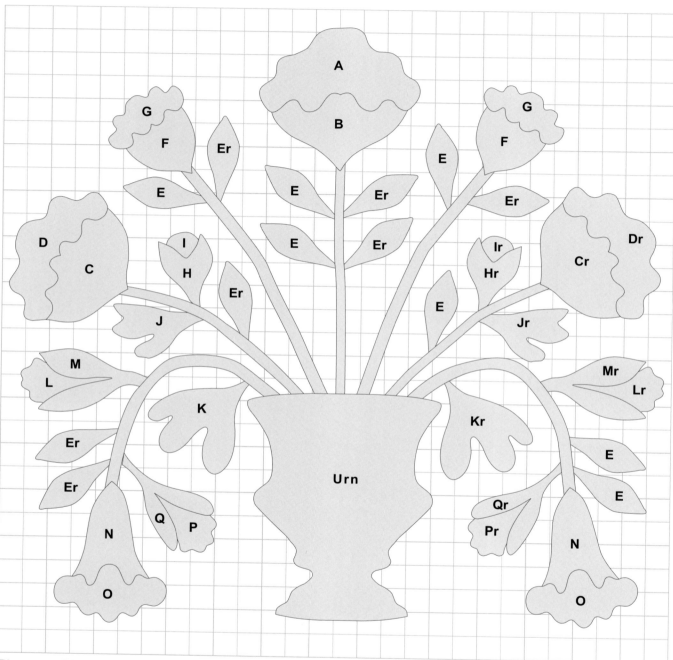

Placement Diagram – Each square =1"

The Coxcomb

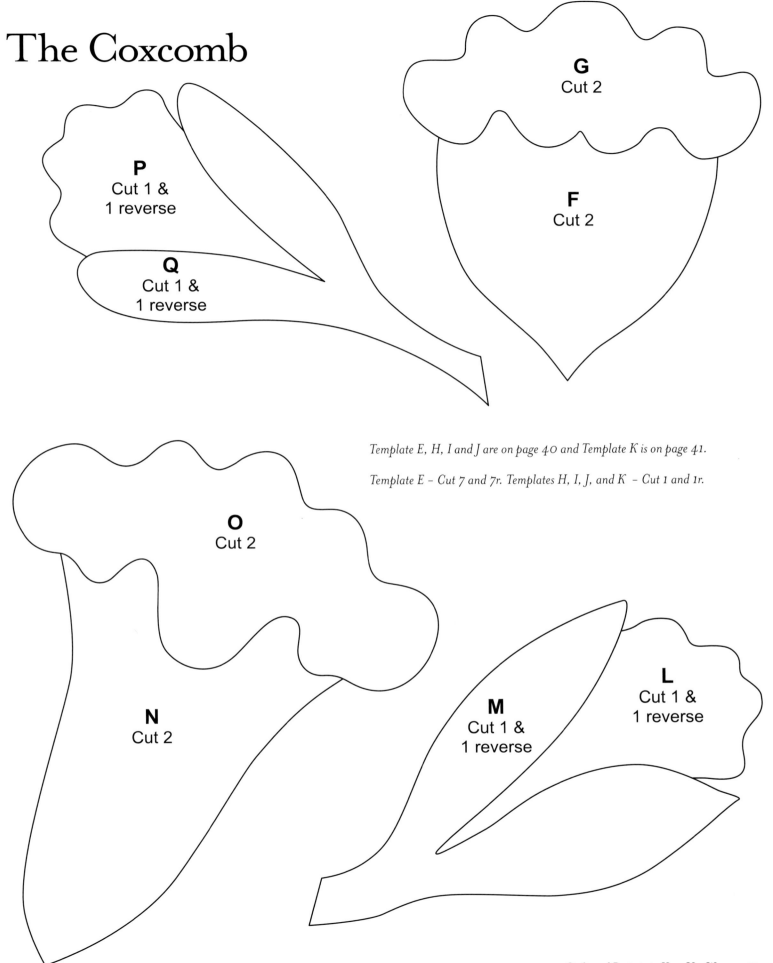

P
Cut 1 &
1 reverse

Q
Cut 1 &
1 reverse

G
Cut 2

F
Cut 2

O
Cut 2

N
Cut 2

M
Cut 1 &
1 reverse

L
Cut 1 &
1 reverse

Template E, H, I and J are on page 40 and Template K is on page 41.

Template E – Cut 7 and 7r. Templates H, I, J, and K – Cut 1 and 1r.

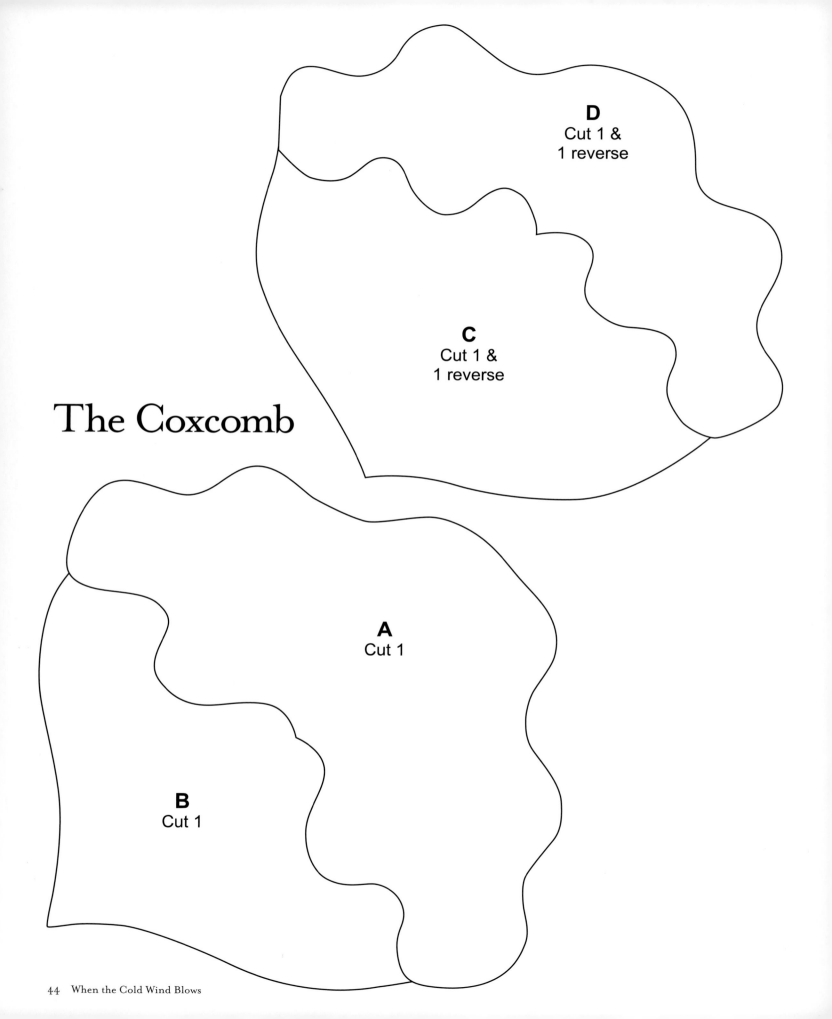

D
Cut 1 &
1 reverse

C
Cut 1 &
1 reverse

The Coxcomb

A
Cut 1

B
Cut 1

The Rose Hip

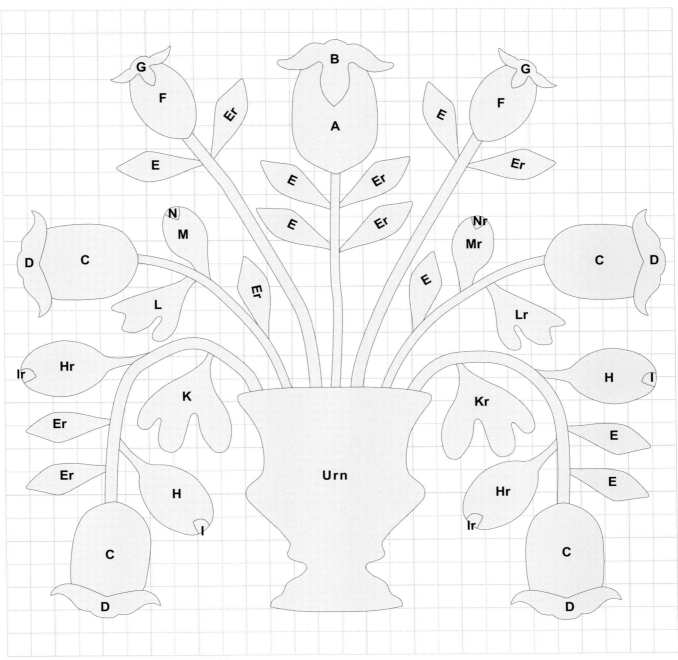

Placement Diagram – Each square =1"

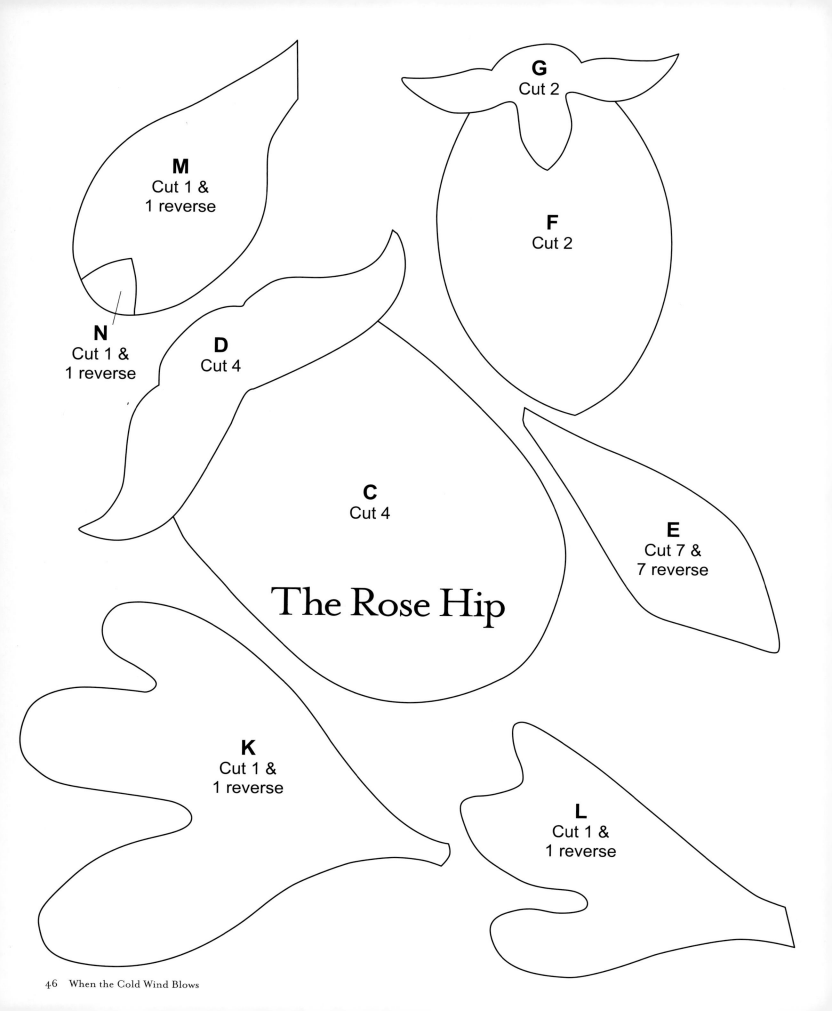

M
Cut 1 &
1 reverse

N
Cut 1 &
1 reverse

D
Cut 4

G
Cut 2

F
Cut 2

C
Cut 4

The Rose Hip

E
Cut 7 &
7 reverse

K
Cut 1 &
1 reverse

L
Cut 1 &
1 reverse

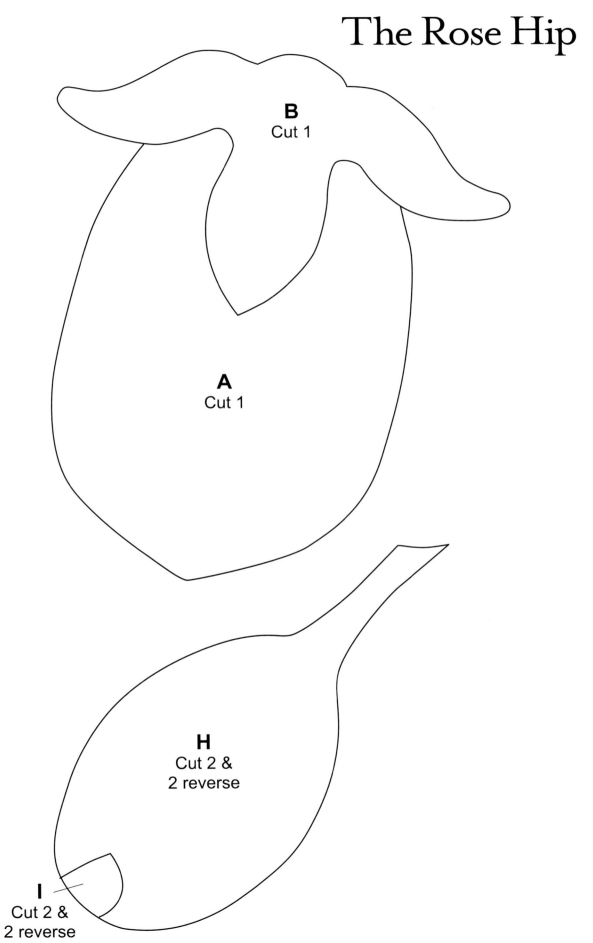

The Rose Hip

B
Cut 1

A
Cut 1

H
Cut 2 &
2 reverse

I
Cut 2 &
2 reverse

The Holly Leaf

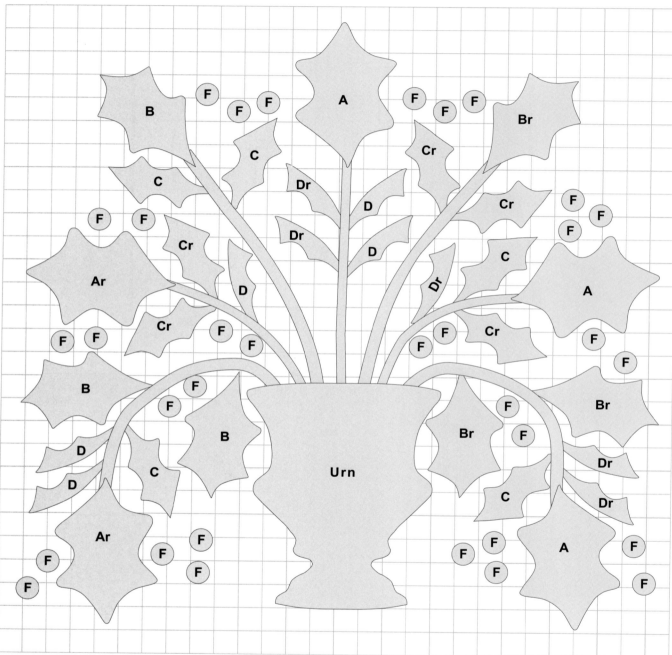

Placement Diagram – Each square =1"

The Holly Leaf

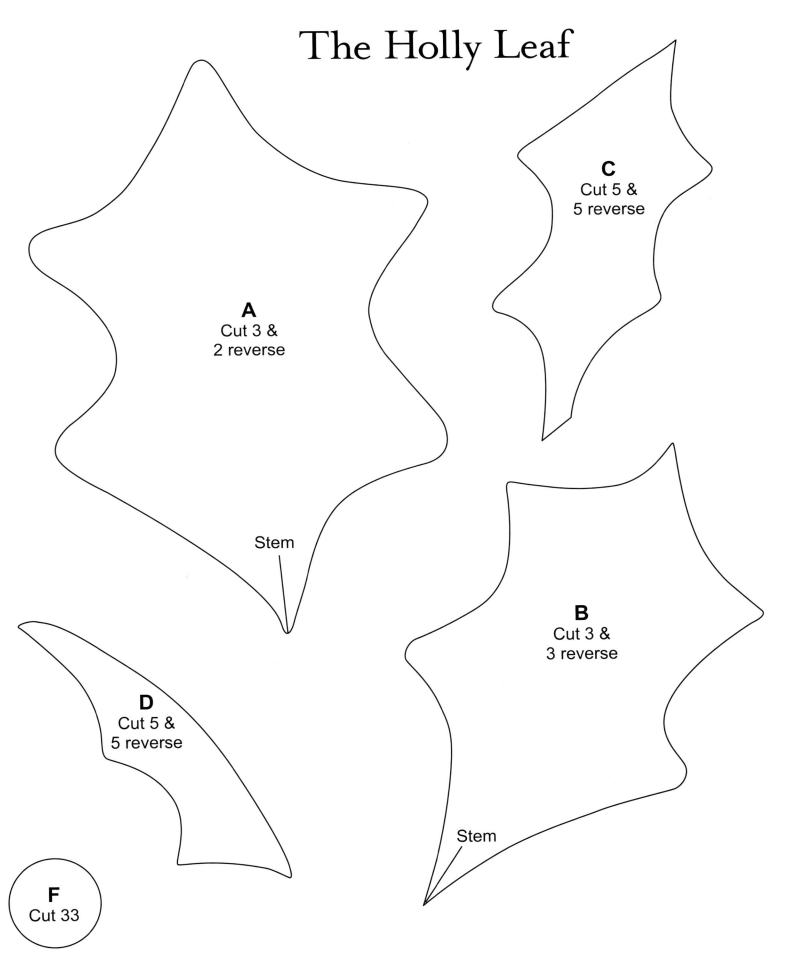

A
Cut 3 &
2 reverse

Stem

C
Cut 5 &
5 reverse

B
Cut 3 &
3 reverse

Stem

D
Cut 5 &
5 reverse

F
Cut 33

The Ornamental Kale

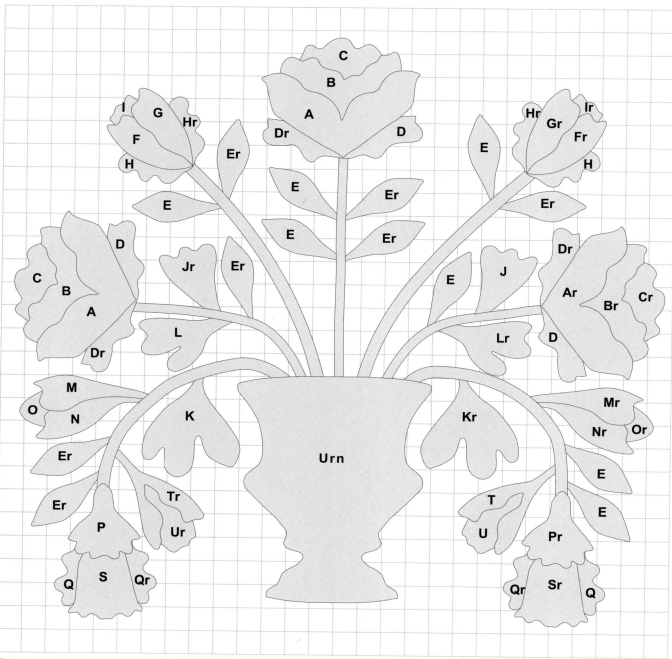

Placement Diagram – Each square =1"

The Ornamental Kale

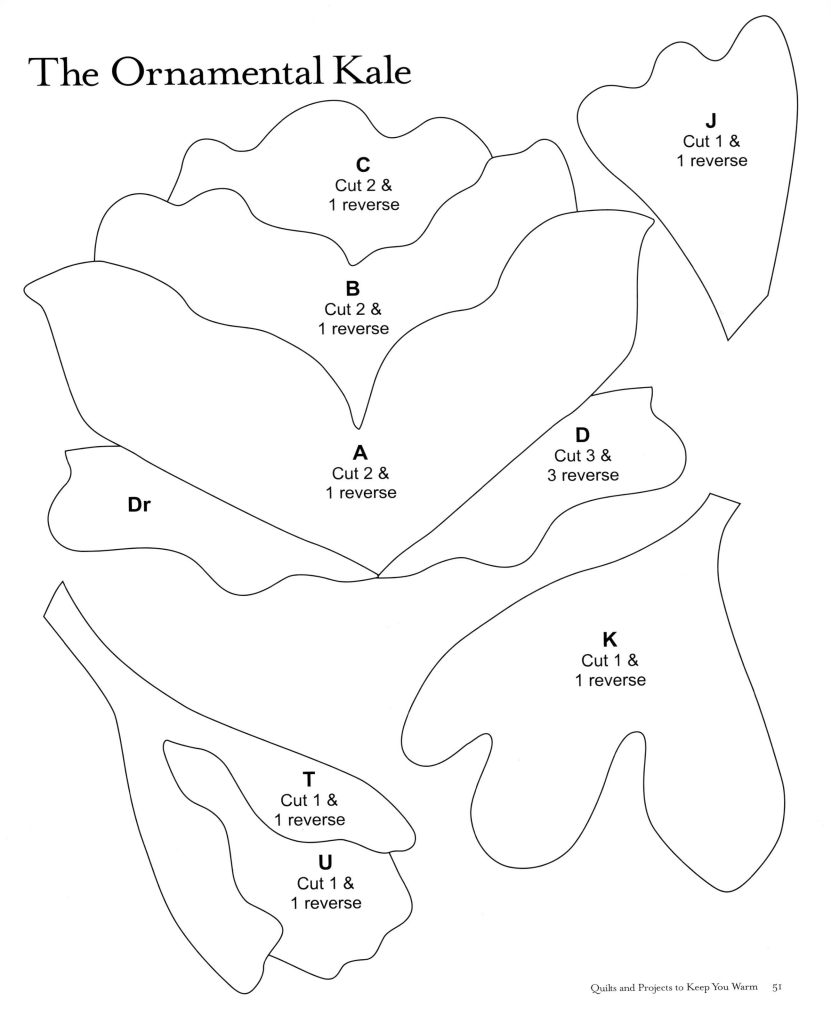

J
Cut 1 &
1 reverse

C
Cut 2 &
1 reverse

B
Cut 2 &
1 reverse

A
Cut 2 &
1 reverse

Dr

D
Cut 3 &
3 reverse

K
Cut 1 &
1 reverse

T
Cut 1 &
1 reverse

U
Cut 1 &
1 reverse

The Ornamental Kale

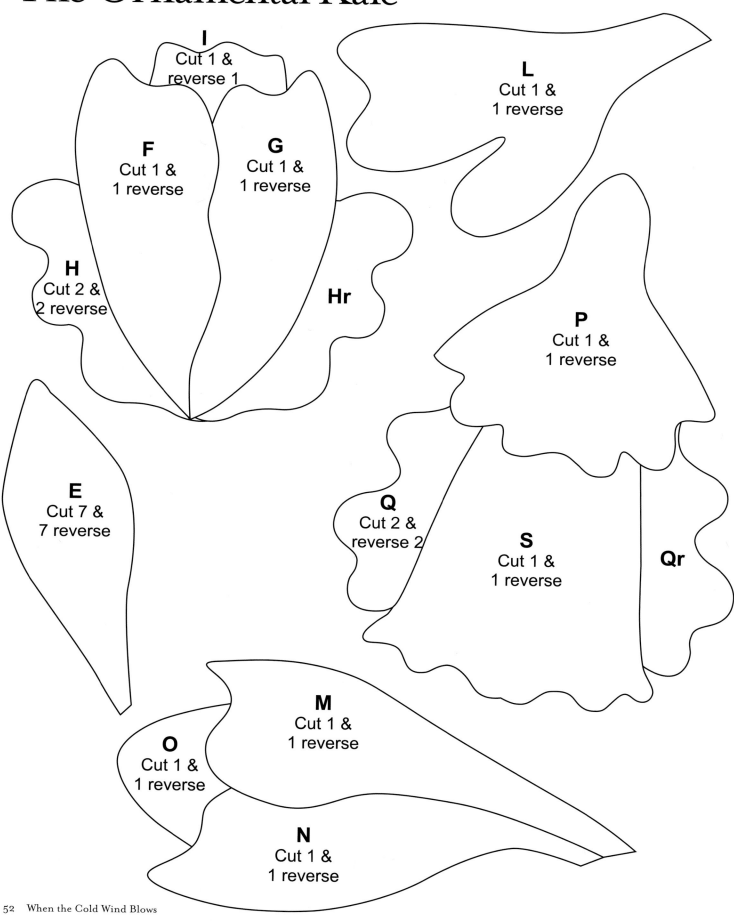

I
Cut 1 &
reverse 1

F
Cut 1 &
1 reverse

G
Cut 1 &
1 reverse

L
Cut 1 &
1 reverse

H
Cut 2 &
2 reverse

Hr

P
Cut 1 &
1 reverse

E
Cut 7 &
7 reverse

Q
Cut 2 &
reverse 2

S
Cut 1 &
1 reverse

Qr

M
Cut 1 &
1 reverse

O
Cut 1 &
1 reverse

N
Cut 1 &
1 reverse

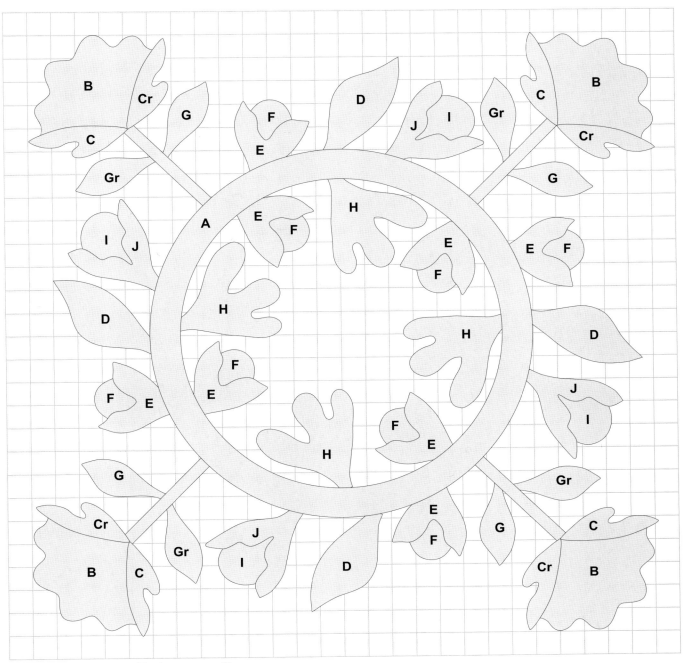

Placement Diagram – Each square =1"

The Winter Wreath

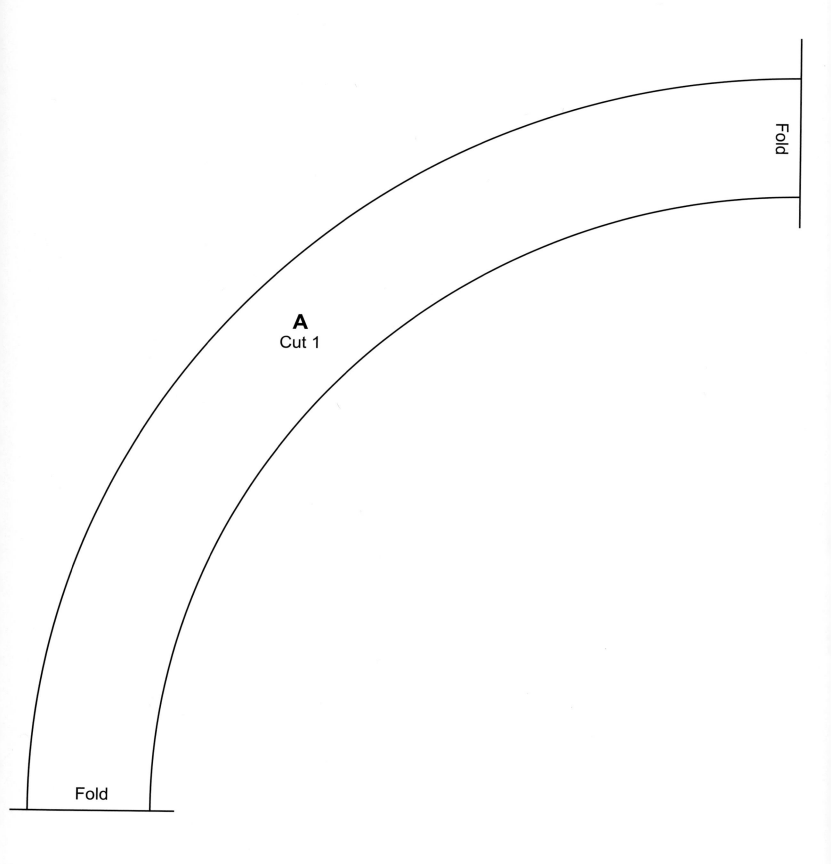

A
Cut 1

Fold

Fold

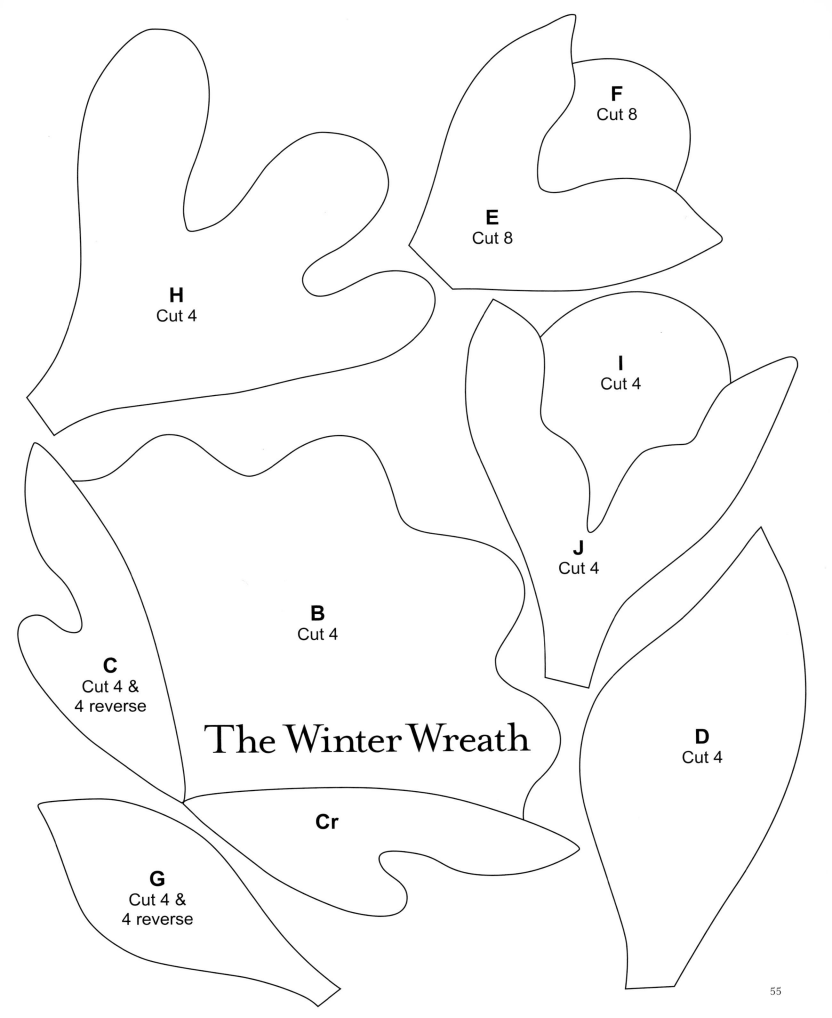

F
Cut 8

E
Cut 8

H
Cut 4

I
Cut 4

J
Cut 4

B
Cut 4

C
Cut 4 &
4 reverse

D
Cut 4

The Winter Wreath

Cr

G
Cut 4 &
4 reverse

The Pomegranate

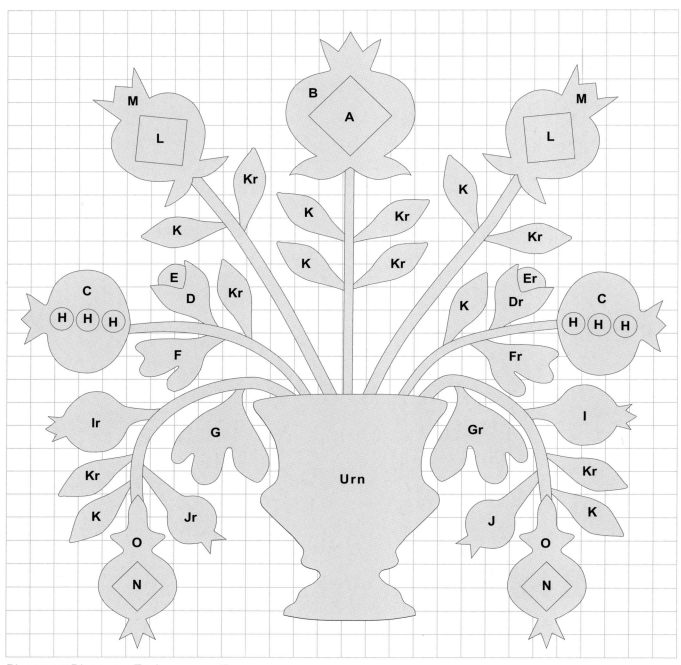

Placement Diagram – Each square =1"

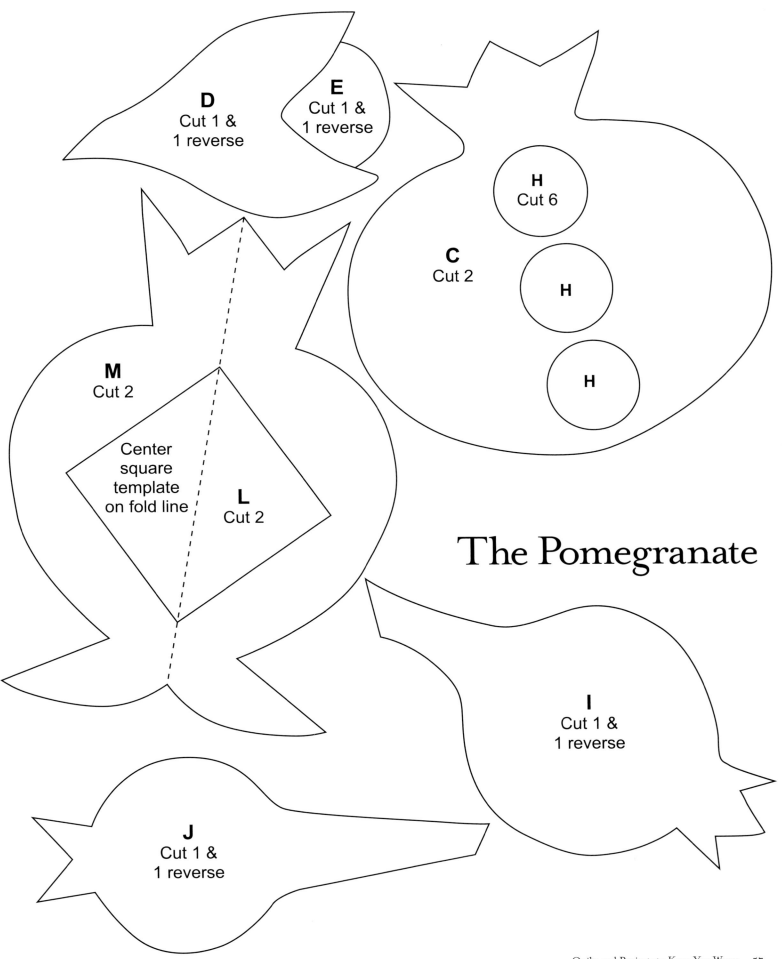

D
Cut 1 &
1 reverse

E
Cut 1 &
1 reverse

H
Cut 6

C
Cut 2

H

H

M
Cut 2

Center
square
template
on fold line

L
Cut 2

The Pomegranate

I
Cut 1 &
1 reverse

J
Cut 1 &
1 reverse

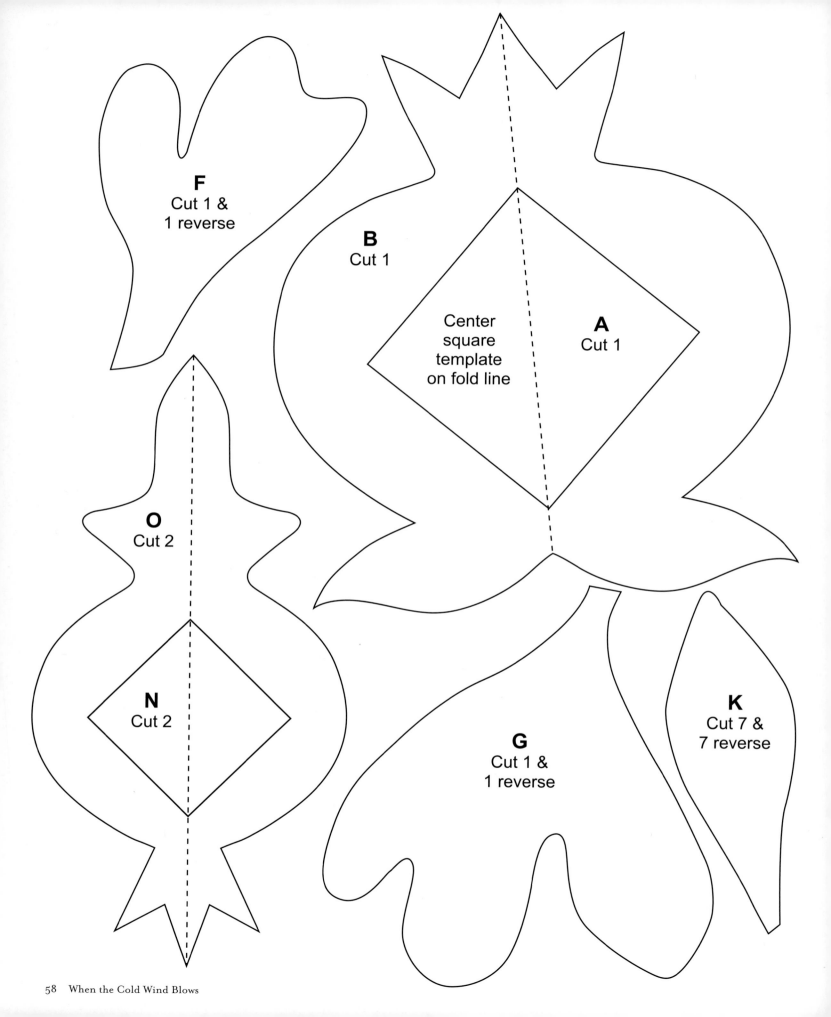

F
Cut 1 &
1 reverse

B
Cut 1

Center
square
template
on fold line

A
Cut 1

O
Cut 2

N
Cut 2

G
Cut 1 &
1 reverse

K
Cut 7 &
7 reverse

Christmas
at Kindred Spirit Place

Ginger Schrader's favorite glass bird

sports an unusual tail.

As you arrive at Ginger and Ron Schrader's home

your eye is drawn to a large cement urn decorated with evergreen boughs, pinecones and large glass balls. Fresh snow is the final garnish. There is something peaceful and magical about visiting this home during the holiday season. Set back from the road on a wooded lot, when you first see their home you feel like you have stepped back in time.

Ginger and Ron both love the look and feel of antique pieces. Their home reflects this love too. After 19 years in their home, they give their collections center stage.

Ron loves reproducing antique lanterns, candleholders and garden cloches. He is a gifted metal worker. His pieces have the look and feel of those made centuries ago.

Ginger's Santa collection began when her twin boys were 3 years old. She noticed two old German cloth Santas at a garage sale. They were

in a box with a sign that said, "Free." Her small boys each asked for one of the Santas, but when Ginger returned home, she told her boys they were Christmas decorations and they couldn't play with them. Old German cloth Santas are now probably worth about $150.00 each. After this find, she began earnestly looking for them at sales. Ginger says they were readily available at the time but are very hard to find now. She then began to reproduce chalkware Santas. She has painted hundreds of these wonderful Santas, much loved by people who have had a chance to purchase one from her.

Every holiday season Ginger decorates her home differently from the previous season. "I love to challenge myself," she says. "The beauty of this peaceful season inspires me."

When walking the property before they built their home, Ginger felt a kinship to their land. She named it "Kindred Spirit Place." The spirit of this talented couple shines throughout their home.

Above: A simple evergreen bough decorates Ginger and Ron's front door. Opposite: Ginger's collection of antique glass bird ornaments are perched on a feather tree.

Opposite page: Ginger converted her studio room into a nature and gardening room. The painted hutch contains collections of bird eggs, old books about trees and flowers, small vases and gardening items. Collected flower prints have been framed and hung as a grouping, bringing nature indoors. Above: A tinsel tree holds Ginger's collection of vintage glass ornaments. The old European garden cloche protects a bird's nest that she collected. Right: The kitchen window holds fresh blooms, adding contrast to a snowy day. Below center: The family cat eyes the perching birds that Ginger has placed on a feather tree.

Opposite page: Ginger has set the table for a Christmas party with several close friends. Each place is set with a different brown transferware platter collected by Ginger. The place setting is united by the matching soup tureens. Individual bouquets are made from snow white mums. Vintage napkins add the final touch. Right: Ginger has made chalkware Santas for many years. Some of her favorites are grouped together, watching to see who has been naughty or nice. Below left: A sweet bird perches on a vase of fresh evergreens on the back door, a welcome reminder of what we love best about winter. Below right: One of Ginger's garden plants bloom through the snow.

Autumn Thistle

Design by Alma Allen; sewing by Alma Allen; quilting by Jeanne Zyck

Autumn Thistle

Project Size 85" x 85" • Block Size 20" finished

I loved working on these blocks. The large pieces were easy and quick to make. My friend Cherie Ralston came over for an afternoon of sewing. Her inspiration gave me the idea for this border design. Where would we be without our friends?

I've decided that I'm only going to make wedding quilts. I have lots of children, nieces and nephews who are going to be getting married soon. I need to begin making something for all of them. So, whoever gets married next is getting this one.

Instructions

Cutting measurements include a 1/4" seam allowance.

- Cut 9 - 20 1/2" squares from the background prints. This will be enough for all of the blocks.

- Make 10 yds. of 1/2" bias tape for the flower stems. This will be enough for all 9 blocks and the border vines. Each flower stem uses a 2" piece of bias tape.

The Thistle Block

- Locate the placement diagram on page 71. Note the templates needed for this block. The templates are located on page 70. Refer to the photo for color placement.

- Cut four 2" long pieces of 1/2" bias tape for the flower stems.

- Cut out the shapes, adding a 1/8" - 1/4" seam allowance. Refer to the diagram and baste the pieces in place on the background fabric.

- Appliqué the pieces to the background.

- Repeat for 9 blocks. Sew the blocks together.

Supply List

For backgrounds

- 3 yds. of a light print for background and border triangles
- 2 5/8 yds. of a light check for background and borders
- 5/8 yd. each of 2 light prints

For appliqué pieces

- Fat quarter each of 4 different blue prints
- Fat quarter each of 4 different tan prints
- 1/2 yd. each of 3 different red prints
- Fat quarter each of 2 different red prints
- Fat quarter each of 4 different plum prints
- Scraps of darker plum fabrics
- 1/8 yd. of gold print
- 3/4 yd for binding
- 9 1/2 yds. jumbo rick rack 1" white (United Notions 454 M & J Trimming)
- 1 bottle Rit dye #16 tan
- 1/2" Clover bias tape maker
- Freezer paper for templates

The Borders

❋ Cut 12 - 6 1/4" squares from 3 red prints. Cut each square in half twice on the diagonal. You will now have 48 red triangles.

❋ Cut 13 - 6 1/4" squares from a light print. Cut each square in half twice on the diagonal. You will now have 52 light triangles.

❋ Sew a strip of 13 light and 12 red triangles. Repeat for 3 more borders. Sew one border to each side of the quilt top. Refer to the picture for color placement.

❋ Cut 4 borders 8" x 65 1/2" from the check print.

❋ Locate the placement diagram on page 69. Note the templates needed for the borders. The templates are located on page 71. Refer to the photo for color placement.

❋ Use the 1/2" bias tape for the vine. Position the vine along the border in a whimsical fashion. Repeat for the remaining 3 borders.

❋ Cut out the shapes, adding a 1/8" - 1/4" seam allowance. Refer to the diagram and baste the pieces in place.

❋ Appliqué the pieces to the borders.

❋ Cut 4 - 8" squares from the light print.

❋ Sew one border to each side of the quilt top.

❋ Sew one 8" square to each end of the two remaining borders. Sew one completed border to the top and one to the bottom of the quilt top.

❋ Cut 17 - 6 1/4" squares from 3 red prints. Cut each square in half twice on the diagonal. You will now have 68 red triangles.

❋ Cut 16 - 6 1/4" squares from a light print. Cut each square in half twice on the diagonal. You will now have 64 light triangles.

❋ Sew a strip of 17 red and 16 light triangles. Repeat for 3 more borders. Sew one border to each side of the quilt top. Refer to the picture for color placement.

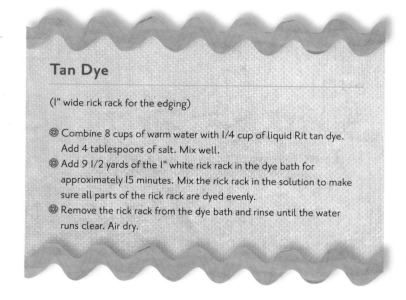

Tan Dye

(1" wide rick rack for the edging)

❋ Combine 8 cups of warm water with 1/4 cup of liquid Rit tan dye. Add 4 tablespoons of salt. Mix well.

❋ Add 9 1/2 yards of the 1" white rick rack in the dye bath for approximately 15 minutes. Mix the rick rack in the solution to make sure all parts of the rick rack are dyed evenly.

❋ Remove the rick rack from the dye bath and rinse until the water runs clear. Air dry.

The Rick Rack Binding

❋ Refer to the dyeing instructions for the rick rack.

❋ Quilt the quilt before sewing the rick rack in place. Baste the rick rack along the right side of the quilt top continuing around each edge. Add a bit of extra rick rack as you baste around each corner. Clip if needed. When you come back to the place you began, fold the raw rick rack edges over into the seam allowance and overlap the rick rack a bit.

❋ Cut bias strips 1 1/2" wide from the binding fabric. Sew them together until you have 10 1/2 yds. Use this strip for your binding. Sew the binding in place, right side of the strip facing the right side of the quilt top. The rick rack will be sandwiched between the quilt top and the binding. Fold the binding over to the back of the quilt, turn under a seam allowance and whip stitch in place.

Autumn Thistle

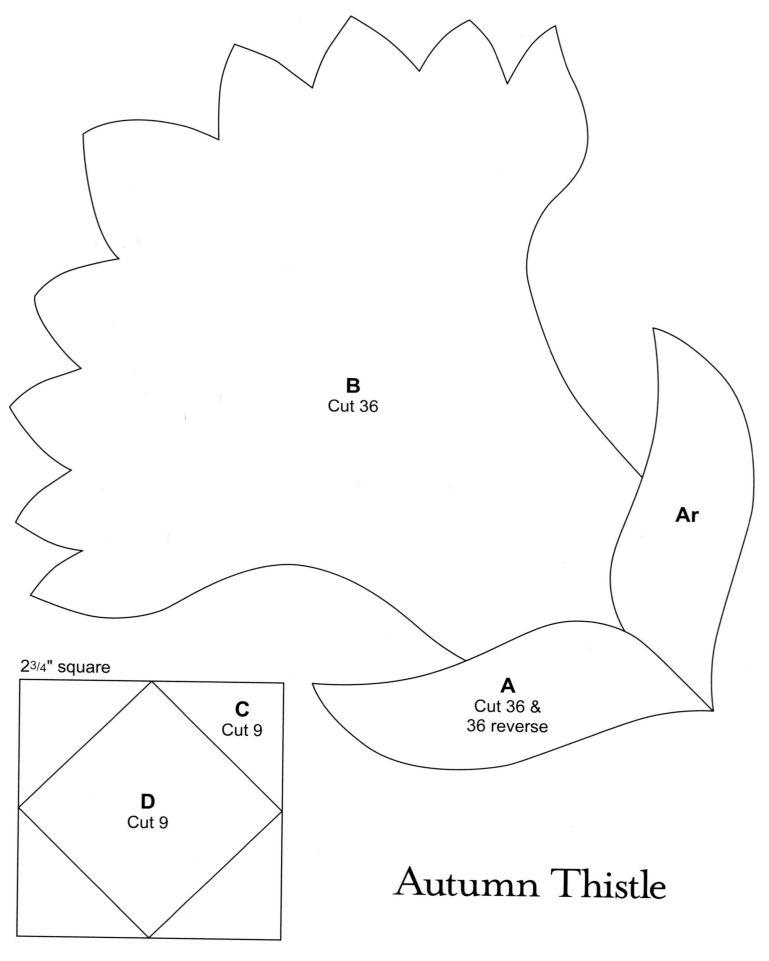

B
Cut 36

Ar

2³/₄" square

C
Cut 9

A
Cut 36 &
36 reverse

D
Cut 9

Autumn Thistle

Harvest Basket

Project Size 83 3/4" x 83 3/4"

Block Size 21 1/4" finished

This quilt began as a collaborative project with Susan Stiff at Moda Fabrics. I drew a design and e-mailed it to Susan. She then recreated the quilt design using a program called Adobe Illustrator. After she created the drawing, I was given a fabric swatch image file to add fabric to the quilt drawing. I was amazed by how much this process helped with color selection. By placing the fabric images in her computerized drawing, I could "try out" pieces and see how the quilt would look before any real fabric was cut and sewn. What a help! This makes me think all quilts should begin this way. With this design method, the best fabric choice is only a few "clicks" away.

Instructions

All measurements given for cutting blocks and pieces in the instructions include a 1/4" seam allowance.

Basket - Appliqué Blocks

For all 5 basket blocks:

- Refer to the Basket and Square-in-a-Square diagram on page 80.

- Cut 3 - 12 7/8"squares for piece K from the tan check print. Cut each in half once on the diagonal. One triangle is needed for each block. Set the remaining triangle aside.

- Cut 10 - 11 1/2" squares for piece J from the assortment of blue prints. Cut each in half on the diagonal once. Four triangles are needed for each block. Set the remaining triangle aside.

For each basket block:

- Cut 9 - 3 7/8" squares from one red print for piece L.

- Cut 5 - 3 7/8 squares from one light tan print for piece L.

Supply List

Numbers refer to "Harvest Home" by Blackbird Designs for Moda fabrics

- 1 yd. large scale blue print (2620-14)
- 1 yd. each of 4 different blue prints (2621-14, 2624-14, 2627-14 & 2628-14)
- 1/4 yd. blue check (2622-14)
- 1/4 yd. blue print (2623-14)
- 2 1/3 yds. large scale plum print for the border (2620-17)
- 1/3 yd. of a plum print (2624-17)
- 1/3 yd. each of 2 bark prints (2626-12 & 2621-12)
- 1/4 yd. each of 2 different green prints for the stems and leaves (2624-15 & 2625-15)
- 1/2 yd. each of 4 different red prints for baskets, bird and border triangles (2621-16, 2626-16, 2627-16 & 2620-16)
- Fat quarter of a solid red fabric (2629-16)
- 1/2 yd. of a tan check for the basket blocks (2622-11)
- 1/3 yd. each of 3 different tan prints for the basket blocks (2628-11, 2623-11 & 2624-11)
- 1/4" Clover bias tape maker

- Cut 1 - 3 1/2" square from a tan print for piece N.

- Cut 4 red print 3 7/8" squares in half once on the diagonal and set these aside for the basket block. The remaining red and tan 3 7/8" squares will be sewn together into red/tan half-square triangle units.

- Place one tan and one red print 3 7/8" square, right sides together, for a red/tan half-square triangle unit. Draw a diagonal line down the center of the light square. Sew two seams, each 1/4" from the marked center line. Cut the two units apart on the drawn line. The result is 2 red/tan half-square triangle units. Repeat for a total of 10 red/tan half-square triangle units. Set one half-square triangle unit aside.

- Refer to the sewing diagram on page 80 and sew the basket base together.

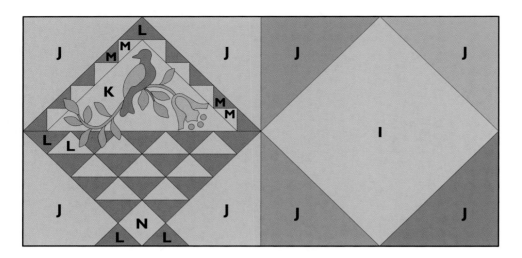

Basket and Square-in-a-Square diagram

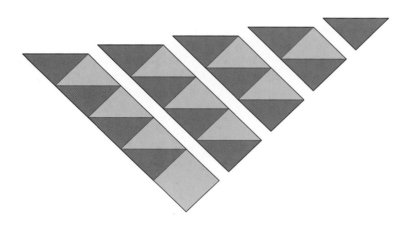

Basket sewing diagram

For each basket foot or J-L combination:

❀ Refer to the basket foot diagram below:

Step 1: Position one of the 3 7/8" red triangles on top of one of the large blue triangles. This is just to see where the seam allowance needs to be.

Step 2: Flip the red triangle over and draw the 1/4" seam allowance on the reverse side. Fold the seam allowance to the back and crease.

Step 3: Again align the red triangle on top of the blue one.

Step 4: Hold the seam allowance in position, and unfold the rest of the red triangle, so the right sides of both triangles are together. Sew along the drawn line.

Step 5: Trim and press. Repeat 1-5 for the opposing blue triangle. Note the placement will be different for the opposite side.

❀ Sew both J/L units to the basket base.

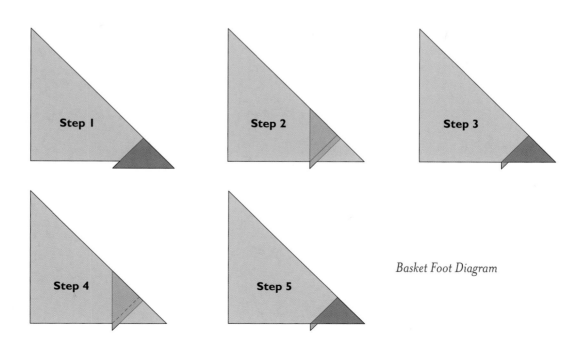

Basket Foot Diagram

For each basket handle:

⊛ Cut 4 - 3" squares each from the red and tan prints for piece M. Cut each in half once on the diagonal. Refer to the sewing diagram and stitch 4 red and 4 tan print triangles together to form one basket handle. Repeat for the remaining side.

⊛ Sew one strip to each side of piece K.

⊛ Center and sew 1 red piece L to the top of the basket handle unit.

⊛ Sew 1 piece J to each side of the basket handle unit.

⊛ Sew the basket handle unit to the basket base to complete the block. Repeat the steps for 5 basket blocks.

Appliqué

⊛ Locate the placement diagram on page 82. Note the templates needed for this block. The templates are located on page 82. Refer to the photo for color placement.

⊛ Make 1 2/3 yd. of 1/4" bias tape for the flower stems. This is enough for all 5 blocks. Each block uses 12" of bias tape.

⊛ Cut out the shapes, adding a 1/8" - 1/4" seam allowance. Refer to the diagram and baste the pieces in place on the block.

⊛ Appliqué the pieces to the block. Repeat for the remaining blocks.

Square-in-a-Square Block

⊛ Cut 4 - 15 1/2" squares from the large scale blue print for piece I.

⊛ Cut 8 - 11 1/2" squares from an assortment of plum and bark prints for piece J. Cut each square in half on the diagonal once.

⊛ Refer to the diagram and piece 4 square-in-a-square blocks. Refer to the sewing diagram and sew the 9 blocks together.

Flying Geese Border

⊛ Cut 144 - 2 1/2" x 4 1/2" rectangles from an assortment of blue prints.

⊛ Cut 296 - 2 1/2" squares from an assortment of red prints. Set aside 8 for the corners.

⊛ Draw a diagonal line from one corner to the opposite corner on each of the 286 squares.

⊛ Place a square, right side down, on one end of the 2 1/2" x 4 1/2" rectangle. Align the edges of both pieces.

⊛ Sew a seam on the drawn line, trim and press. Repeat for the remaining side of the rectangle. Refer to the diagram on the left.

⊛ Assemble 144 Flying Geese units.

⊛ Sew 4 strips of 16 each. Sew one strip each to 2 sides of the quilt.

⊛ Sew one 2 1/2" red print square to each end of the remaining 2 strips. Sew one strip to the top and one to the bottom of the quilt.

Fabric Border

⊛ Cut 2 strips 6 1/2" x 68 1/4" from the large scale plum print.

⊛ Sew one strip to each side of the quilt.

⊛ Cut 2 strips 6 1/2" x 80 1/4" from the large scale plum print. Sew one strip to the top and one to the bottom of the quilt.

Final Flying Geese Border

⊛ Sew 4 strips of 20 each. Sew one strip each to 2 sides of the quilt.

⊛ Sew one 2 1/2" red print square to each end of the remaining 2 strips. Sew one strip to the top and one to the bottom of the quilt.

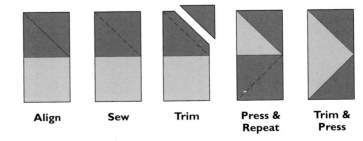

Align **Sew** **Trim** **Press & Repeat** **Trim & Press**

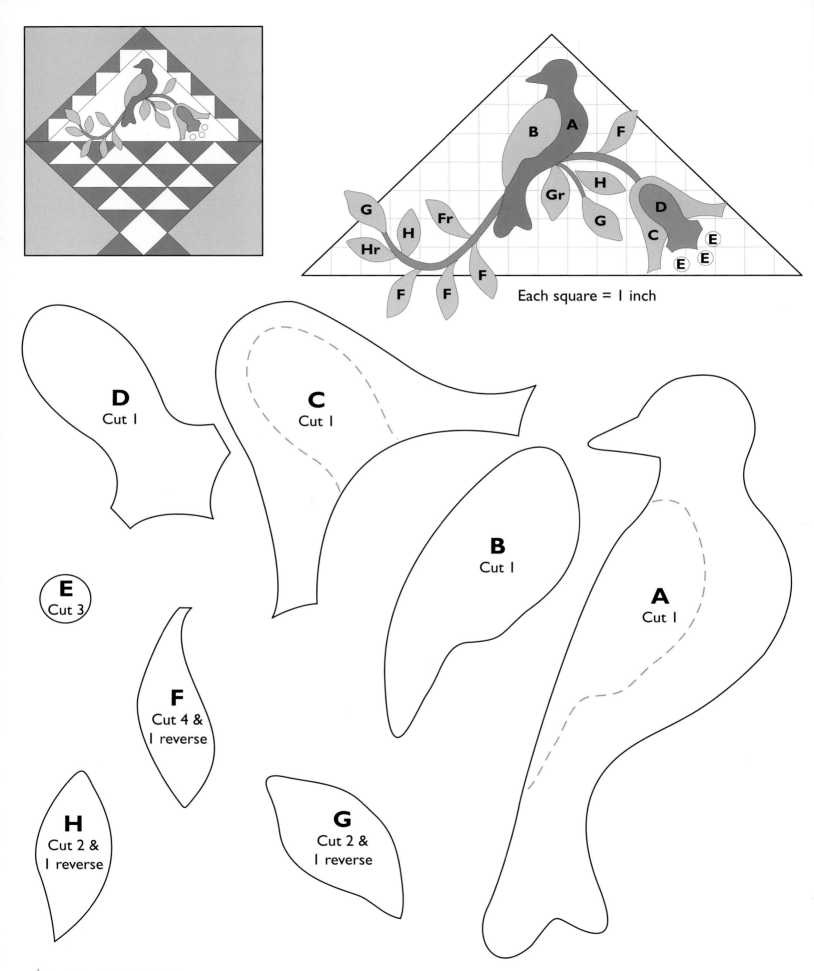

Each square = 1 inch

D
Cut 1

C
Cut 1

E
Cut 3

B
Cut 1

A
Cut 1

F
Cut 4 &
1 reverse

H
Cut 2 &
1 reverse

G
Cut 2 &
1 reverse

Sewing Diagram

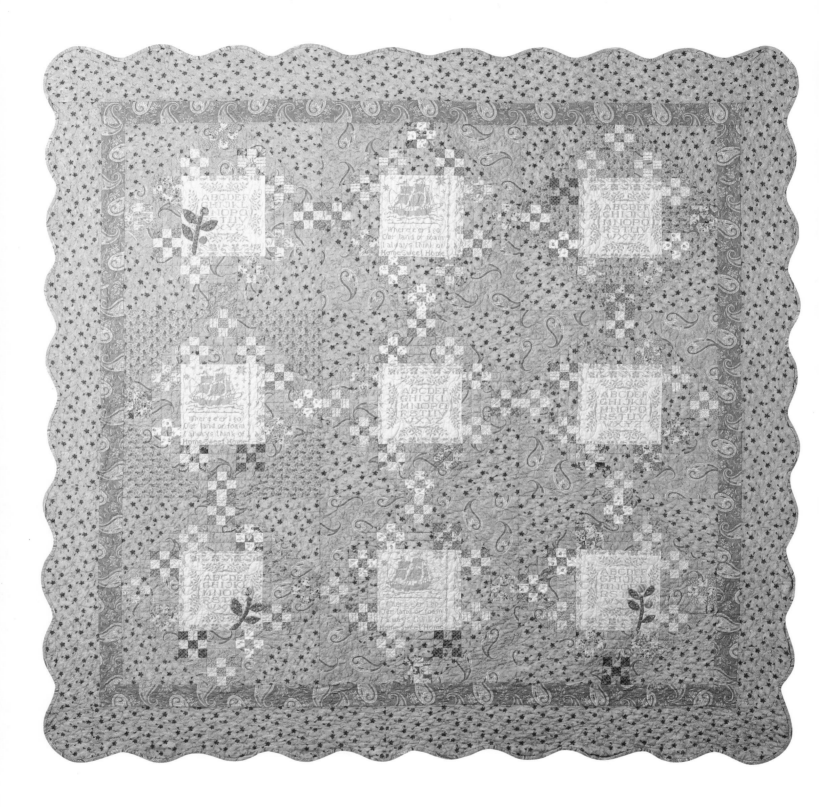

Goldenrod in Bloom

Design by Alma Allen; sewing by Alma Allen; quilting by Jean Zyck

Goldenrod in Bloom

Project Size 80" x 80" • Block Size 21" finished

When the nights begin to cool in September, the Goldenrod, a native perennial, begins to flower. Roadsides and fallow fields begin to turn yellow with bloom. This tall, prairie flower is in the Aster family.

Goldenrod has falsely been blamed for allergic reactions. Really it's quite harmless. Most allergies during this time of the year are due to Ragweed.

Pieced Block Instructions

All measurements given for cutting blocks and pieces in the instructions include a 1/4" seam allowance.

⚜ Cut 48 - 1 1/2" squares from an assortment of light prints.

⚜ Cut 60 - 1 1/2" squares from an assortment of dark green, light green, light blue, and pink prints.

⚜ Piece 12 nine-patch blocks. Refer to the picture for color placement.

⚜ Cut 4 - 3 1/2" squares from the yellow and pink paisley print.

⚜ Cut 6 - 3 7/8" squares from the yellow and pink paisley print. Cut each square in half on the diagonal once.

⚜ Cut 1 - 9 1/2" square from the light sampler print or another light print you have chosen.

⚜ Cut 2 - 9 7/8" squares from the yellow and pink floral print. Cut each in half once on the diagonal.

⚜ Refer to the Block Sewing Diagram and piece one block.

⚜ Repeat for 9 blocks. To give a scrappy look, alternate the position of the yellow and pink paisley print and the yellow and pink floral prints with the remaining blocks.

Supply List

⚜ 2 1/2 yds. yellow and pink floral print for second border and pieced blocks
⚜ 2 yds. yellow and pink paisley print for binding and pieced blocks
⚜ 1/3 yd. of a different yellow and pink floral print
⚜ 1 1/2 yd. sampler print (more is needed for special cut) or 7/8 yd. of another light print
⚜ 2 yds. pink paisley print for first border and pieced blocks
⚜ 1/8 yd. each of 7 different light prints
⚜ 1/8 yd. each of a dark green, light green, light blue, and 4 different pink prints
⚜ 1/8 yd. tan and green print for appliqué

Appliqué Instructions

Three of the blocks have an appliquéd flower stem.

⚜ Locate the placement diagram on page 89. Note the templates needed for this block. The templates are located on page 89. Refer to the photo for color placement.

⚜ Cut out the shapes, adding a 1/8" - 1/4" seam allowance. Refer to the diagram and baste the pieces in place on the 3 blocks.

⚜ Appliqué the pieces to the blocks.

⚜ Sew the 9 blocks together.

Border Instructions

- Cut 2 strips 3" x 63 1/2" from the pink paisley print. Sew one strip to each side of the quilt.

- Cut 2 strips 3" x 68 1/2" from the pink paisley print. Sew one strip to the top and one to the bottom of the quilt.

- Cut 2 strips 6 1/2" x 68 1/2" from the yellow and pink floral print. Sew one strip to each side of the quilt.

- Cut 2 strips 6 1/2" x 80 1/2" from the yellow and pink floral print. Sew one strip to the top and one to the bottom of the quilt.

- Use freezer paper to make the scallop template. Cut a piece 86" long. Trace the scallop template on the freezer paper. Align and continue to trace until you have a corner scallop and 8 side scallops. End the strip with another corner scallop. Set the template aside.

- Quilt the top before cutting the scallops. The quilting design keeps the fabric border from stretching after the scallops are cut. The scallop border design is drafted for an 80" long border. The quilting takes up the fabric and reduces the length of the border. To adjust for the change in size of your quilted border, make small folds in the paper template along the flat, inside curve to reduce its length. These small adjustments in the template are not noticeable in the finished quilt.

- Pin the template in place. Cut along the edge of the template. Repeat for the remaining sides.

- Cut 2 1/4" bias strips from the yellow and pink paisley print for the binding. Make 10 yards of binding. Fold the binding in half. Match the selvedge edges of the binding to the raw edge on the top side of the quilt. Sew the binding to the quilt top. Do not pull the binding fabric tightly along the top edge of the scallop. Turn the binding over to the back of the quilt and blind stitch in place.

Goldenrod in Bloom

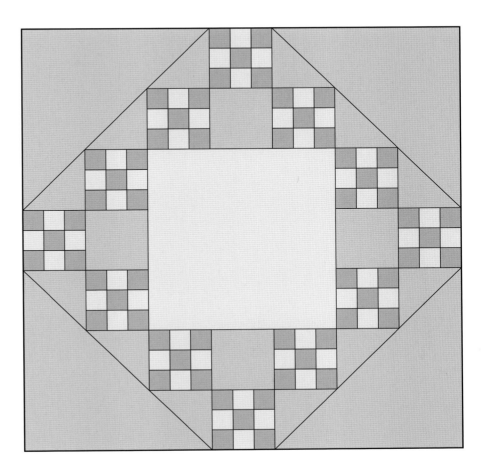

Block Sewing Diagram

Goldenrod in Bloom

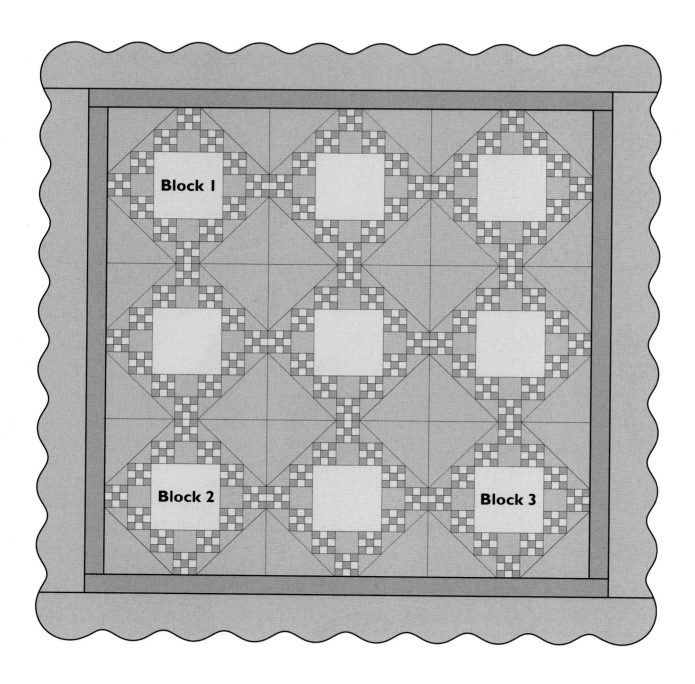

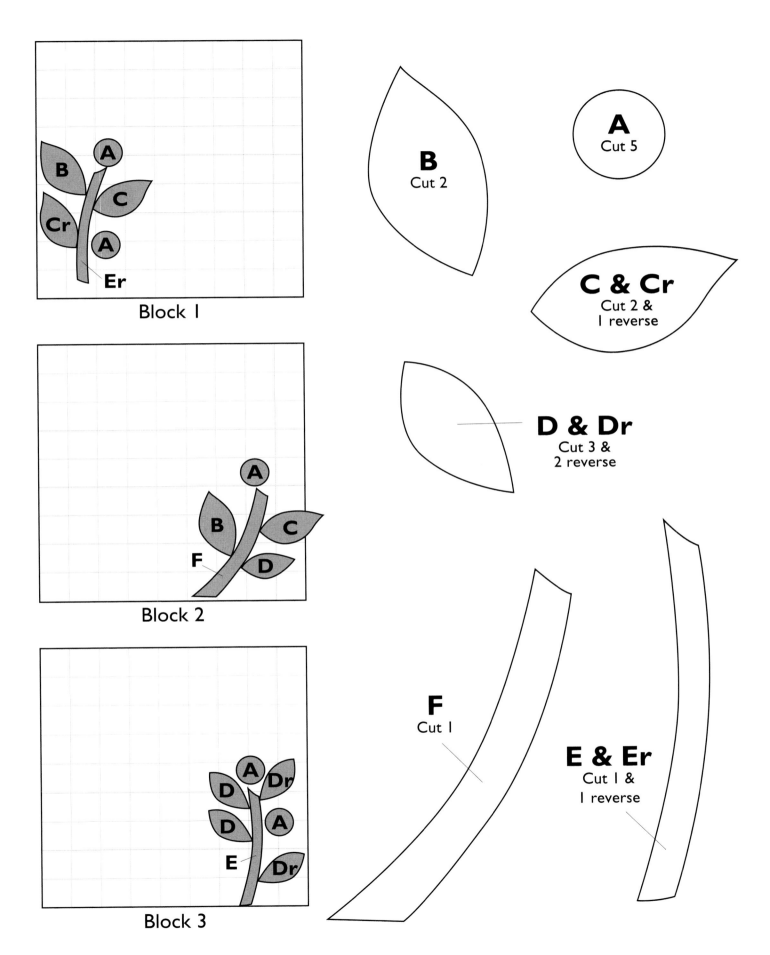

Block 1

Block 2

Block 3

B
Cut 2

A
Cut 5

C & Cr
Cut 2 &
1 reverse

D & Dr
Cut 3 &
2 reverse

F
Cut 1

E & Er
Cut 1 &
1 reverse

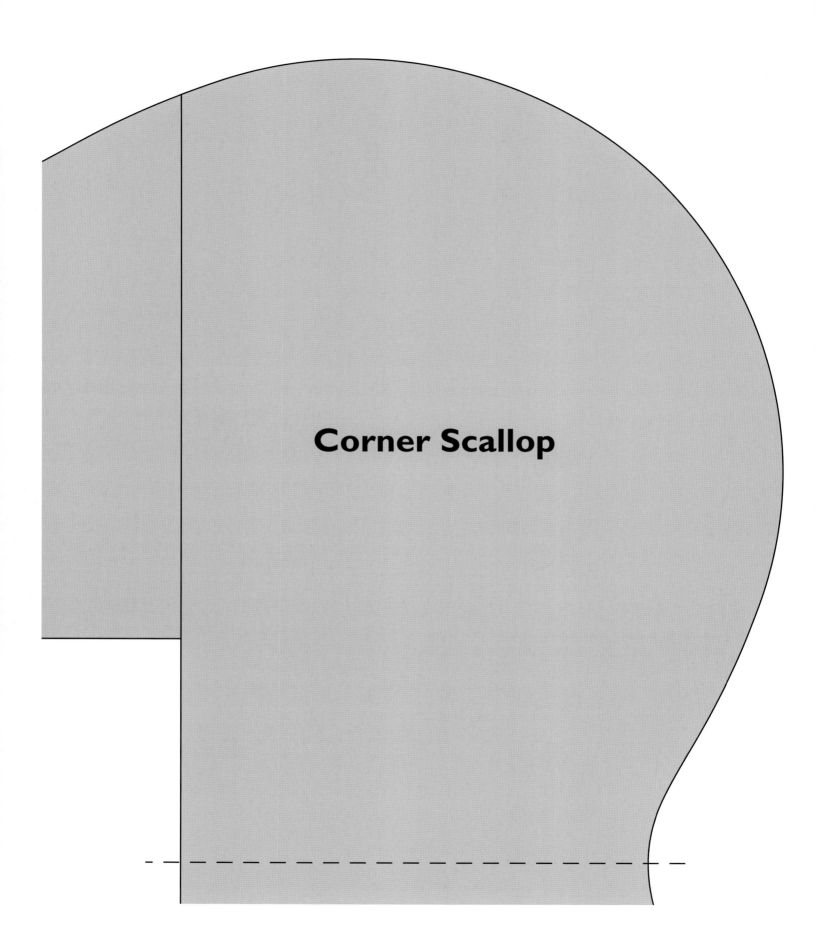

Corner Scallop

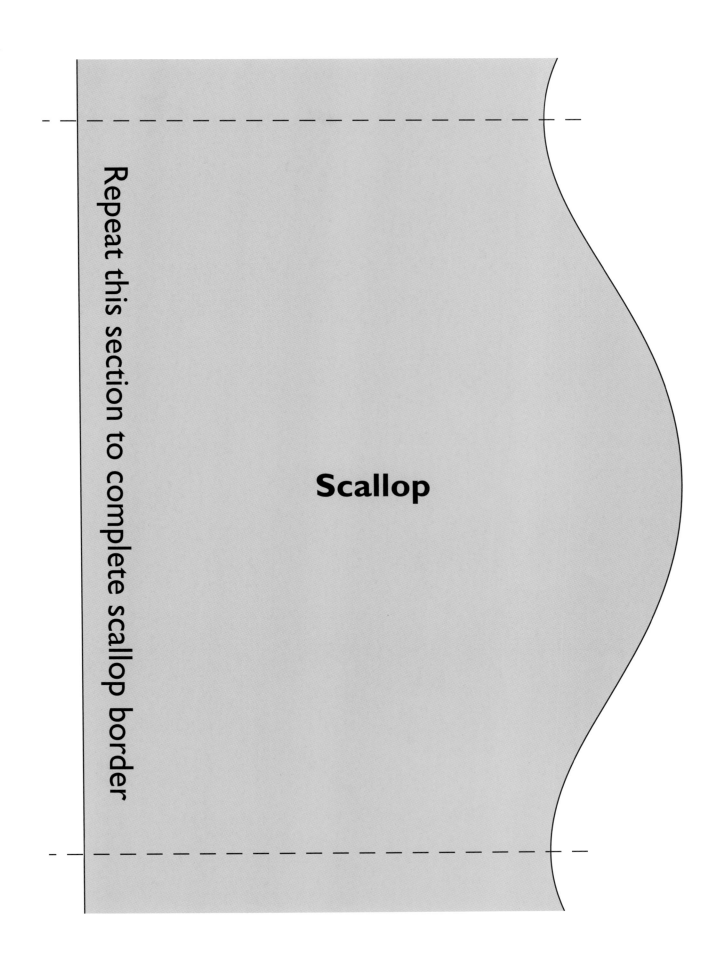

Repeat this section to complete scallop border

Scallop

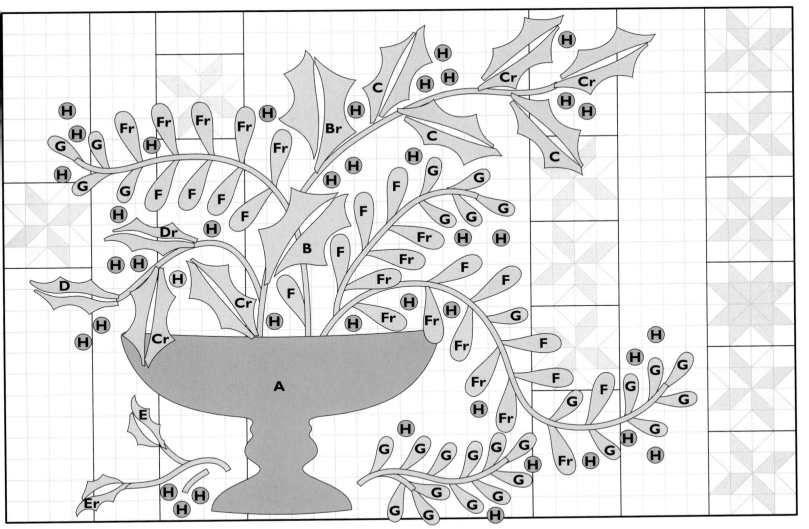

Appliqué Block D Placement Diagram

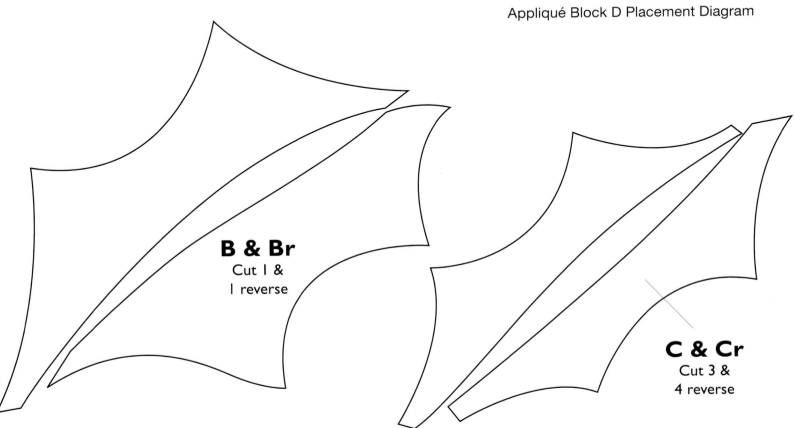

B & Br
Cut 1 &
1 reverse

C & Cr
Cut 3 &
4 reverse

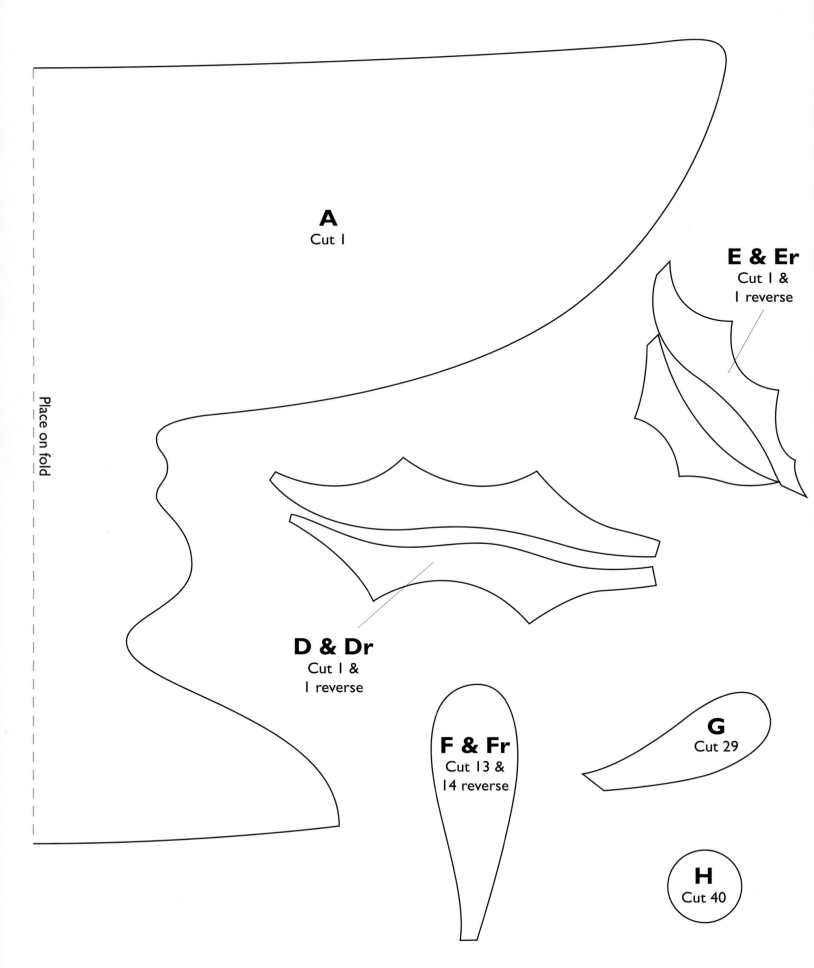

A
Cut 1

Place on fold

E & Er
Cut 1 &
1 reverse

D & Dr
Cut 1 &
1 reverse

F & Fr
Cut 13 &
14 reverse

G
Cut 29

H
Cut 40

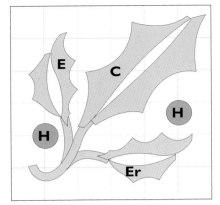

Block E

Template C
Cut 1

Template E
Cut 1 & 1 reverse

Template H
Cut 2

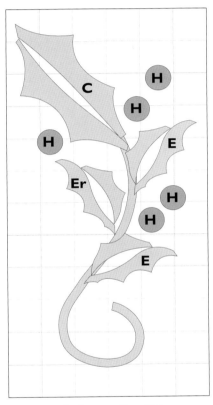

Block F

Template C
Cut 1

Template E
Cut 2 & 1 reverse

Template H
Cut 5

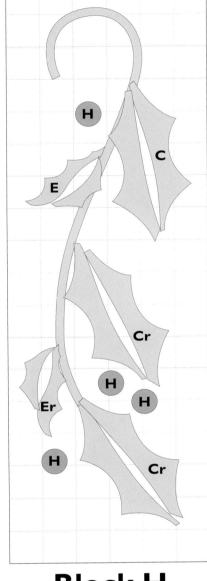

Block H

Template C
Cut 1 & 2 reverse

Template E
Cut 1 & 1 reverse

Template H
Cut 4

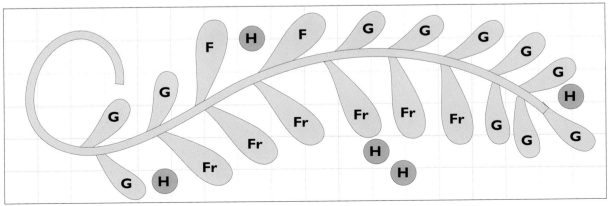

Block G

Template G
Cut 11

Template F
Cut 2 & 6 reverse

Template H
Cut 5

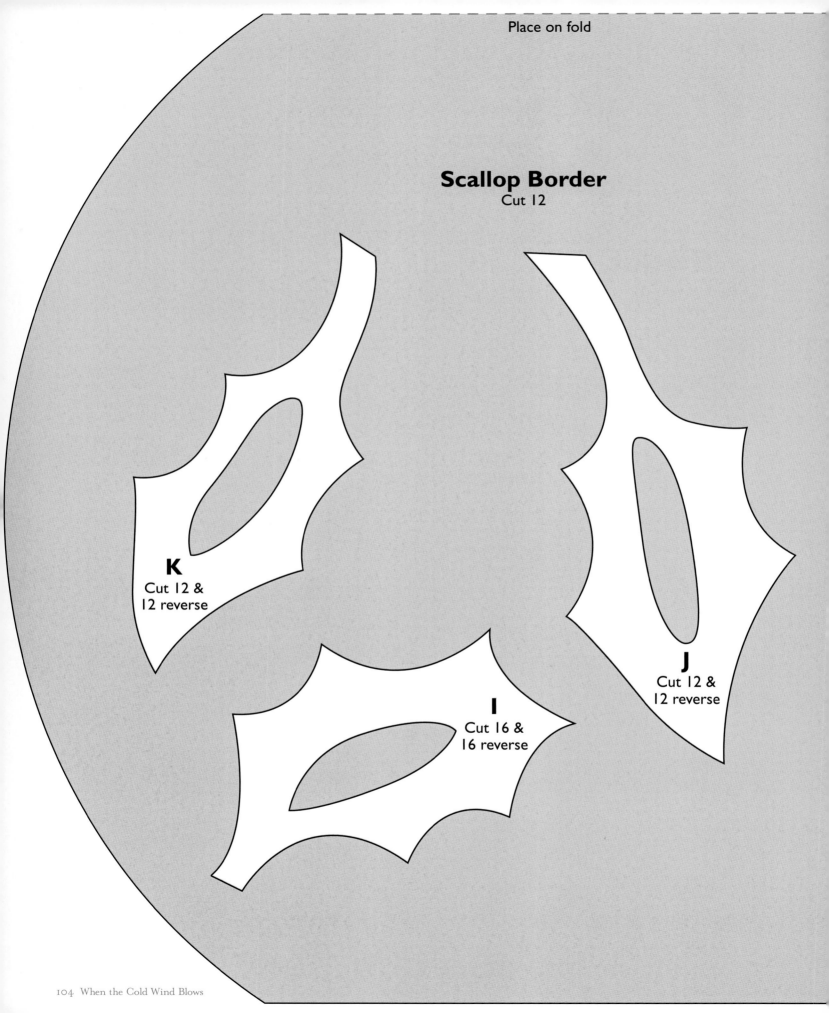

Scallop Border
Cut 12

K
Cut 12 &
12 reverse

J
Cut 12 &
12 reverse

I
Cut 16 &
16 reverse

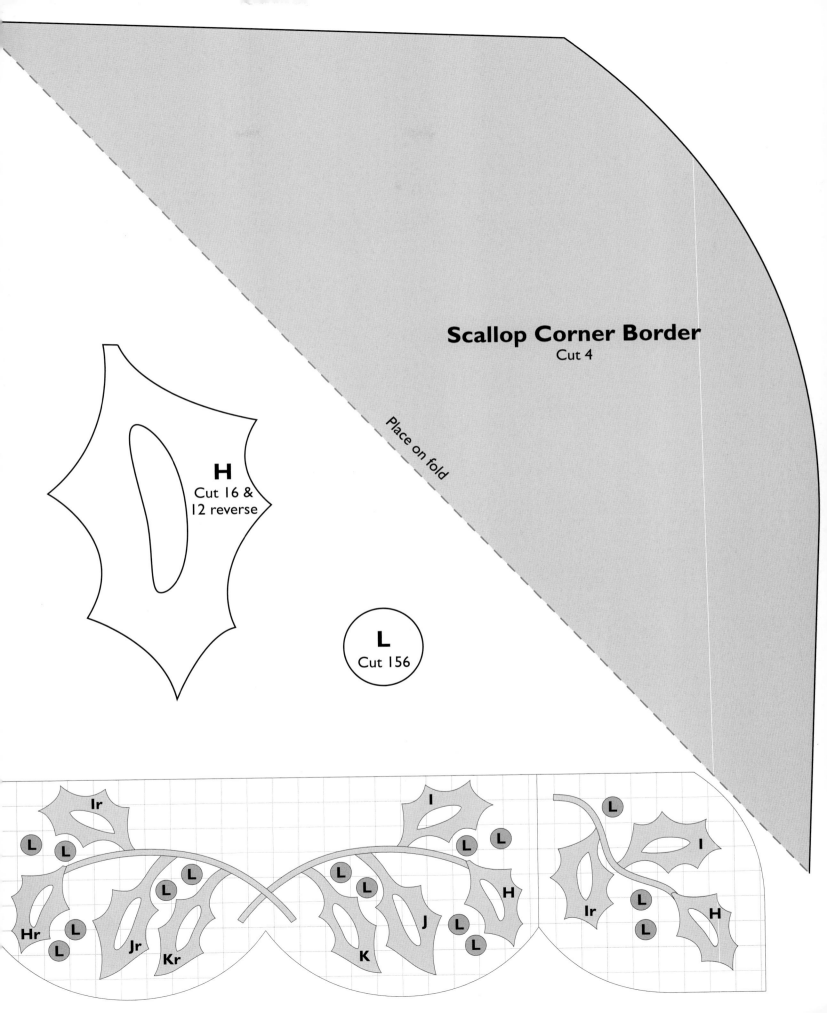

Scallop Corner Border
Cut 4

Place on fold

H
Cut 16 &
12 reverse

L
Cut 156

Frost on the Ferns

Project Size 51" x 51"

Barb used the templates from the Coxcomb block in the featured quilt for this wonderfully dramatic piece. She left out one of the leaves on the flower stem and added the blue birds. With a color palette change, adding the fern border and blue birds, a whole new look is achieved.

Instructions

The Center Block

Cutting measurements include a 1/4" seam allowance.

🌼 Cut 1 - 28 1/2" square from the background fabric.

🌼 Locate the placement diagram on page 109. Note the templates needed for this block. The templates are located on pages 33, 43 and 44. Refer to the photo for color placement.

🌼 Make 3/4 yd. of 3/8" bias tape and 1/1/4 yds. of the 1/2" bias tape for the center block.

🌼 Cut out the shapes, adding a 1/8" - 1/4" seam allowance. Refer to the diagram and baste the pieces in place on the background fabric.

🌼 Appliqué the pieces to the background.

First Border

🌼 Refer to the dyeing instructions on page 108 and dye the rick rack.

🌼 Cut 2 - 2" x 28 1/2" strips from the background fabric.

🌼 Cut 2 lengths of rick rack 28 1/2" long. Refer to the picture for placement and appliqué the dyed rick rack length along one edge of the fabric strip. Repeat for the remaining strip. Sew the rick rack border to each side of the quilt top.

🌼 Cut 2 - 2" x 31 1/2" strips from the background fabric.

🌼 Cut 2 lengths of rick rack 31 1/2" long. Appliqué the dyed rick rack to the 2 strips as before. Sew one rick rack border to the top and one to the bottom of the quilt top.

Supply List

The fabric numbers refer to the "Harvest Home" line of fabrics by Blackbird Designs for Moda Fabrics.

For background

🌼 2 yds. of a solid purple kale fabric (2622-17)

For appliqué pieces

🌼 1/3 yd. of milkweed print (2624-11)
🌼 Fat quarter each of 5 different milkweed prints (2628-11, 2623-11, 2626-11, 2627-11 & 2625-11)
🌼 Fat quarter of a purple kale print (2622-17)
🌼 Fat quarter each of 2 front porch blue paint prints (2628-14, 2623-14)
🌼 5/8 yd. for the binding
🌼 9 yds. jumbo cotton rick rack 1" white (United Notions 454 M & | Trimming)
🌼 1 bottle of Rit Dye #16 Tan
🌼 1 package of dry Rit Dye #42 Golden Yellow
🌼 Salt
🌼 3/8" and 1/2" Clover bias tape maker

Pieced Blocks

🌼 Cut 4 - 3 3/8" squares each from two blue prints. Cut each on the diagonal once.

🌼 Cut 8 - 3 3/8" squares from a milkweed print. Cut each on the diagonal once.

🌼 Cut 8 - 3 3/8" squares from a purple kale print. Cut each on the diagonal once.

🌼 Cut 8 - 3" squares from a purple kale print for corner units. Refer to the sewing diagram and piece two star blocks. Set these aside.

Side Borders

◈ Cut 2 - 10 1/2" x 31 1/2" strips from the background fabric.

◈ Locate the placement diagram on page 109. Note the templates needed for these border strips. The templates are located on page 111. Refer to the photo for color placement.

◈ Make 5 yards of 3/8" bias tape from a milkweed print for the ferns. This will be enough for all borders. Whimsically place the vine along the border and cut the length of vine needed from the 5 yd. piece.

◈ Cut out the shapes, adding a 1/8" - 1/4" seam allowance. Refer to the diagram and baste the pieces in place on the background fabric.

◈ Appliqué the pieces to each border strip.

◈ Sew one border to each side of the quilt.

Center Bottom Border

◈ Cut a 10 1/2" x 31 1/2" strip from the background fabric.

◈ Locate the placement diagram on page 109. Note the templates needed for this border strip. The templates are located on page 111. Refer to the photo for color placement.

◈ Cut the length of 3/8" bias tape needed for this border.

◈ Cut out the shapes, adding a 1/8" - 1/4" seam allowance. Refer to the diagram and baste the pieces in place on the border strip.

◈ Appliqué the pieces to the border strip.

◈ Sew one pieced-star block on each end of this strip. Sew the strip to the bottom of the quilt.

Top Border

◈ Cut a 10 1/2" x 51 1/2" strip from the background fabric.

◈ Locate the placement diagram on page 109. Note the templates needed for this border strip. The templates are located on pages 43 and 111. Refer to the photo for color placement.

◈ Cut the length of 3/8" bias tape needed for this border.

◈ Cut out the shapes, adding a 1/8" - 1/4" seam allowance. Refer to the diagram and baste the pieces in place on the border strip.

◈ Appliqué the pieces to the border strip.

◈ Sew this border to the top of quilt.

The Rick Rack Binding

◈ Quilt the quilt before sewing the rick rack in place. Baste the rick rack along the right side of the quilt top continuing around each edge. Add a bit of extra rick rack as you baste around each corner. Clip if needed. When you come back to the place you began, fold the raw rick rack edges over into the seam allowance and overlap the rick rack a bit.

◈ Cut bias strips 1 1/2" wide from the binding fabric. Sew them together until you have 6 yds. Use this strip for your binding. Sew the binding in place with the right side of the strip, facing the right side of the quilt top. The rick rack will be sandwiched between the quilt top and the binding. Fold the binding over to the back of the quilt, turn under a seam allowance and whip stitch in place.

Tan Dye

(1" wide rick rack for the edging)

◈ Combine 8 cups of warm water with 1/4 cup of liquid Rit tan dye and 1/4 teaspoon of golden yellow powder dye. Add 4 tablespoons of salt. Mix well.

◈ Add 9 yards of the 1" white rick rack in the dye bath for approximately 15 minutes. Mix the rick rack in the solution to make sure all parts of the rick rack are dyed evenly.

◈ Remove the rick rack from the dye bath and rinse until the water runs clear. Air dry.

Frost on the Ferns

Placement Diagram

Frost on the Ferns

Design by Barb Adams; sewing by Leona Adams; quilting design by Jeanne Zyck

Frost on the Ferns

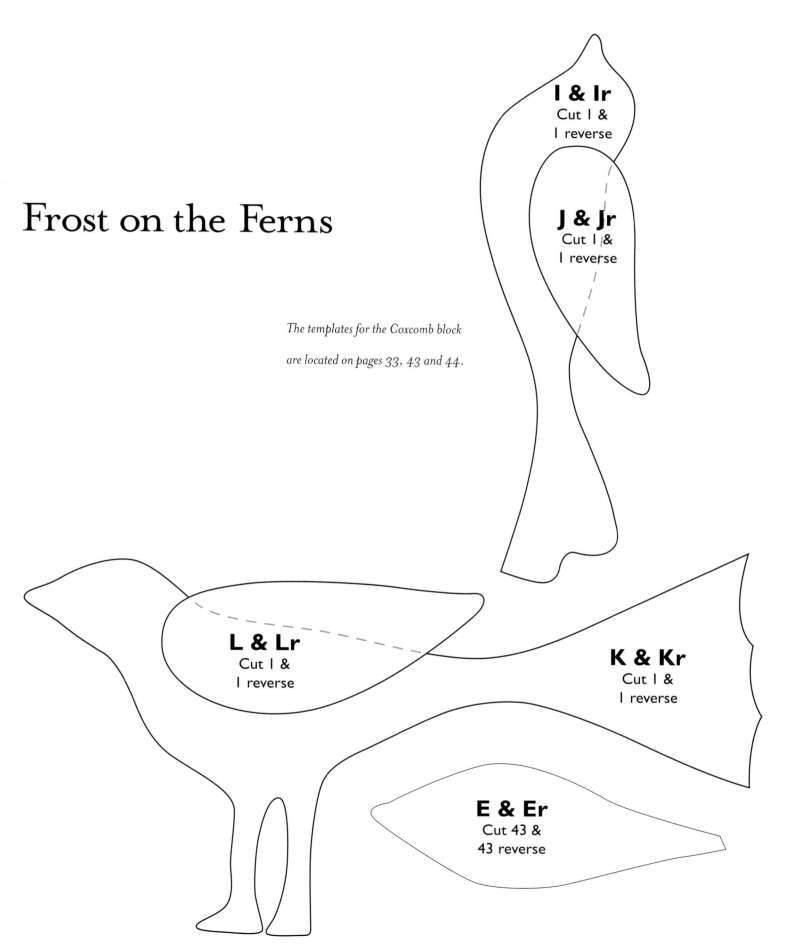

The templates for the Coxcomb block

are located on pages 33, 43 and 44.

I & Ir
Cut 1 &
1 reverse

J & Jr
Cut 1 &
1 reverse

L & Lr
Cut 1 &
1 reverse

K & Kr
Cut 1 &
1 reverse

E & Er
Cut 43 &
43 reverse

'Back to School' Pillow Sham

Design by Barb Adams; sewing by Leona Adams

Rose Hip Hooked Rug

Project Size 24" x 20"

Instructions

❀ Cut the rug linen 32" x 28".

❀ Sew around the edge of the rug linen with the zig-zag stitch on your sewing machine to prevent fraying.

❀ Draw the design on red dot tracer or nylon organdy. Center the red dot tracer or nylon organdy on the linen. Retrace the design with a Sharpie permanent marker. The ink from the marker will bleed through the red dot tracer onto the rug linen.

❀ Cut the strips for the stems and rose hips with a #8 blade. (About 1/4" wide.) Cut the strips for the leaves with a #6 blade. Cut the background strips with a #8 1/2 blade.

❀ Outline and hook the shapes first.

❀ After the shapes are filled, begin hooking the background following the contours of the pattern. For a smooth appearance, outline the shapes with the background color. Then continue to outline the shapes until they begin to meet. Fill the remaining spaces following a natural flow of hooking.

Finishing Techniques

❀ Dampen a towel and place your finished rug face down on the towel. Iron with a medium setting on your steam iron.

❀ Bind the edges with plum colored yarn.

❀ Trim the edges to 1/2" and sew twill tape over the raw edges.

Supply List

Wool

❀ 12" x 18" peach-rust colored spot-dyed wool for the rose hips
❀ 12" x 18" terra-cotta overdyed wool for the rose hips
❀ 12" x 18" peach-brown plaid for the rose hips
❀ 6" x 18" rust-brown for the rose hips
❀ 1/2 yd. of assorted green for the leaves (Choose shades from yellow-green to dark green.)
❀ 1/2 yd. dark plum spot-dyed wool for the border
❀ 12" x 18" plum tweed for the border
❀ 18" x 18" warm brown for the stems
❀ 1 yd. of assorted cream, tan and taupe plaids and herringbone weaves for the background

Other Supplies

❀ 32" x 28" rug linen
❀ Rug frame and hook
❀ Red dot tracer or nylon organdy
❀ Sharpie permanent marker
❀ Plum yarn for binding
❀ 2 3/4 yds. twill tape for finishing

Rose Hip Hooked Rug

Pattern Layout Diagram

Top Left

Bottom Center

Bottom Left

Bottom Right

Other Star Books

One Piece at a Time by Kansas City Star Books – 1999
More Kansas City Star Quilts by Kansas City Star Books – 2000
Outside the Box: Hexagon Patterns from The Kansas City Star
   by Edie McGinnis – 2001
Prairie Flower: A Year on the Plains by Barbara Brackman – 2001
The Sister Blocks by Edie McGinnis – 2001
Kansas City Quiltmakers by Doug Worgul – 2001
O' Glory: Americana Quilts Blocks from The Kansas City Star
   by Edie McGinnis – 2001
Hearts and Flowers: Hand Appliqué from Start to Finish
   by Kathy Delaney – 2002
Roads and Curves Ahead: A Trip Through Time with Classic Kansas City Star
   Quilt Blocks by Edie McGinnis – 2002
❀ Celebration of American Life: Appliqué Patterns Honoring a Nation and Its
   People by Barb Adams and Alma Allen – 2002
❀ Women of Grace & Charm: A Quilting Tribute to the Women Who Served in
   World War II by Barb Adams and Alma Allen – 2003
A Heartland Album: More Techniques in Hand Appliqué
   by Kathy Delaney – 2003
Quilting a Poem: Designs Inspired by America's Poets
   by Frances Kite and Deb Rowden – 2003
Carolyn's Paper Pieced Garden: Patterns for Miniature and Full-Sized Quilts
   by Carolyn Cullinan McCormick – 2003
Friendships in Bloom: Round Robin Quilts by Marjorie Nelson and Rebecca
   Nelson-Zerfas – 2003
Baskets of Treasures: Designs Inspired by Life Along the River
   by Edie McGinnis – 2003
Heart & Home: Unique American Women and the Houses that Inspire by Kathy
   Schmitz – 2003
Women of Design: Quilts in the Newspaper by Barbara Brackman – 2004
The Basics: An Easy Guide to Beginning Quiltmaking
   by Kathy Delaney – 2004
Four Block Quilts: Echoes of History, Pieced Boldly & Appliquéd Freely
   by Terry Clothier Thompson – 2004
No Boundaries: Bringing Your Fabric Over the Edge by Edie McGinnis – 2004
Horn of Plenty for a New Century by Kathy Delaney – 2004
Quilting the Garden by Barb Adams and Alma Allen – 2004
Stars All Around Us: Quilts and Projects Inspired by a Beloved Symbol
   by Cherie Ralston – 2005
Quilters' Stories: Collecting History in the Heart of America by Deb Rowden
   – 2005
Libertyville: Where Liberty Dwells, There is My Country by Terry Clothier
   Thompson – 2005
Sparkling Jewels, Pearls of Wisdom by Edie McGinnis – 2005
Grapefruit Juice and Sugar: Bold Quilts Inspired by Grandmother's Legacy
   by Jenifer Dick – 2005
❀ Home Sweet Home by Barb Adams and Alma Allen – 2005
Patterns of History: The Challenge Winners by Kathy Delaney – 2005
My Quilt Stories by Debra Rowden – 2005
Quilts in Red and Green and the Women Who Made Them by Nancy Hornback
   and Terry Clothier Thompson – 2006
Hard Times, Splendid Quilts: A 1930s Celebration, Paper Piecing from
   The Kansas City Star by Carolyn Cullinan McCormick – 2006
Art Nouveau Quilts for the 21st Century by Bea Oglesby – 2006
Designer Quilts: Great Projects from Moda's Best Fabric Artists – 2006
❀ Birds of a Feather by Barb Adams and Alma Allen – 2006
Feedsacks! Beautiful Quilts from Humble Beginnings by Edie McGinnis – 2006
Kansas Spirit: Historical Quilt Blocks and the Saga of the Sunflower State by
   Jeanne Poore – 2006

Bold Improvisation: Searching for African-American Quilts – The Heffley
   Collection by Scott Heffley – 2007
The Soulful Art of African-American Quilts: Nineteen Bold, Improvisational
   Projects by Sonie Ruffin – 2007
Alphabet Quilts: Letters for All Ages by Bea Oglesby – 2007
Beyond the Basics: A Potpourri of Quiltmaking Techniques
   by Kathy Delaney – 2007
Golden's Journal: 20 Sampler Blocks Honoring Prairie Farm Life
   by Christina DeArmond, Eula Lang and Kaye Spitzli – 2007
Borderland in Butternut and Blue: A Sampler Quilt to Recall the Civil War Along
   the Kansas/Missouri Border by Barbara Brackman – 2007
Come to the Fair: Quilts that Celebrate State Fair Traditions
   by Edie McGinnis – 2007
Cotton and Wool: Miss Jump's Farewell by Linda Brannock – 2007
❀ You're Invited! Quilts and Homes to Inspire by Barb Adams and Alma Al-
   len, Blackbird Designs – 2007
Portable Patchwork: Who Says You Can't Take it With You?
   by Donna Thomas – 2008
Quilts for Rosie: Paper Piecing Patterns from the '40s
   by Carolyn Cullinan McCormick – 2008
Fruit Salad: Appliqué Designs for Delicious Quilts by Bea Oglesby – 2008
Red, Green and Beyond by Nancy Hornback and Terry Clothier Thompson
   – 2008
A Dusty Garden Grows by Terry Clothier Thompson – 2008
We Gather Together: A Harvest of Quilts by Jan Patek – 2008
With These Hands: 19th Century-Inspired Primitive Projects for Your Home
   by Maggie Bonanomi – 2008
Caring for Your Quilts: Textile Conservation, Repair and Storage by Hallye
   Bone – 2008
The Circuit Rider's Quilt: An Album Quilt Honoring a Beloved Minister by Jeni-
   fer Dick – 2008
Embroidered Quilts: From Hands and Hearts by Christina DeArmond, Eula
   Lang and Kaye Spitzli – 2008
Reminiscing: A Whimsicals Collections by Terri Degenkolb – 2008
Scraps and Shirttails: Reuse, Re-purpose and Recycle! The Art of Green Quilting
   by Bonnie Hunter – 2008

Queen Bees Mysteries:
Murders on Elderberry Road by Sally Goldenbaum – 2003
A Murder of Taste by Sally Goldenbaum – 2004
Murder on a Starry Night by Sally Goldenbaum – 2005
Dog-Gone Murder by Marnette Falley – 2008

Project Books:
Fan Quilt Memories by Jeanne Poore – 2000
Santa's Parade of Nursery Rhymes by Jeanne Poore – 2001
As the Crow Flies by Edie McGinnis – 2007
Sweet Inspirations by Pam Manning – 2007
Quilts Through the Camera's Eye by Terry Clothier Thompson – 2007
Louisa May Alcott: Quilts of Her Life, Her Work, Her Heart by Terry Cloth-
   ier Thompson – 2008
The Lincoln Museum Quilt: A Reproduction for Abe's Frontier Cabin by Barbara
   Brackman and Deb Rowden – 2008
Dinosaurs - Stomp, Chomp and Roar by Pam Manning – 2008
Carrie Hall's Sampler: Favorite Blocks from a Classic Pattern Collection
   by Barbara Brackman – 2008

DVD Projects:
The Kansas City Stars: A Quilting Legacy – 2008